Marketing Logistics

The Marketing Series is one of the most comprehensive collections of books in marketing and sales available from the UK today.

Published by Butterworth-Heinemann on behalf of The Chartered Institute of Marketing, the series is divided into three distinct groups: *Student* (fulfilling the needs of those taking the Institute's certificate and diploma qualifications); *Professional Development* (for those on formal or self-study vocational training programmes); and *Practitioner* (presented in a more informal, motivating and highly practical manner for the busy marketer).

Formed in 1911, The Chartered Institute of Marketing is now the largest professional marketing management body in Europe with over 60,000 members located worldwide. Its primary objectives are focused on the development of awareness and understanding of marketing throughout UK industry and commerce and in the raising of standards of professionalism in the education, training and practice of this key business discipline.

Books in the series

The Marketing Book
Michael J. Baker

Practice of Public Relations
Sam Black

Marketing Logistics
Martin Christopher

Relationship Marketing
Martin Christopher, Adrian Payne and David Ballantyne

Profitable Product Management
Richard Collier

Marketing Research for Managers
Sunny Crouch and Matthew Housden

Creating Powerful Brands
Leslie de Chernatony and Malcolm H. B. McDonald

CIM Marketing Dictionary
Norman A. Hart

Practice of Advertising
Norman A. Hart

Marketing Plans
Malcolm H. B. McDonald

Marketing Planning for Services
Malcolm H. B. McDonald and Adrian Payne

Retail Marketing Plans
Malcolm H. B. McDonald and Christopher Tideman

Relationship Marketing for Competitive Advantage
Adrian Payne, Martin Christopher, Moira Clark and Helen Peck

Market-led Strategic Change
Nigel Piercy

Trade Marketing Strategies
Geoffrey Randall

Below-the-line Production
John Wilmshurst

Marketing Logistics

Published on behalf of
The Chartered Institute of Marketing

Martin Christopher

With case study contributions by

Helen Peck

Butterworth-Heinemann
Linacre House, Jordan Hill, Oxford OX2 8DP
A division of Reed Educational and Professional Publishing Ltd

 A member of the Reed Elsevier plc group

OXFORD BOSTON JOHANNESBURG
MELBOURNE NEW DELHI SINGAPORE

First published 1997

British Library Cataloguing in Publication Data
Christopher, Martin
Marketing logistics
1. Marketing – Management
I. Title II. Chartered Institute of Marketing
658.5

ISBN 0 7506 2209 1

Data manipulation by David Gregson Associates, Beccles, Suffolk
Printed in Great Britain by Biddles Ltd, Guildford and King's Lynn

Contents

Preface

Only recently have many marketing managers come to recognize the importance of 'availability'. This is all the more difficult to comprehend given the lip service paid to the old adage that marketing is all about 'the right product in the right place at the right time'. Yet an examination of the major texts used on most undergraduate and graduate business programmes finds little detailed analysis of the concepts of logistics or the practical realities involved in serving customers better at less cost. Worse still the marketing plans of some of the best-known companies also seem to take distribution related issues for granted.

The good news is that there are signs of a growing realization that, for many organizations, customer service provides one of the few ways in which they can differentiate themselves in a world of 'me-toos', lookalikes and clones.

The fusion of marketing and logistics that provides the focus for this book should be a critical component of overall business strategy, not something that stands alone subject to a quite separate management and planning responsibility.

The recurrent theme of this book is that customers and consumers have become more demanding of the service they receive from supplying organizations. Coincident with this pressure is the trend towards market 'maturity' that leads to a decline in brand loyalty and a tendency towards what might be described as 'commodity' markets. In other words, customers are less likely to be influenced by conventional marketing appeals but more by such issues as availability, speed of response and supplier support.

The conclusion that must be drawn from these trends is that logistics needs to move higher up the agenda in debates about marketing strategy within the business. It is with this in mind that this book was conceived and written.

Inevitably, in preparing this book I have drawn upon numerous sources and benefited from the ideas of many of my colleagues at Cranfield and elsewhere. I am particularly indebted to Helen Peck who has contributed most of the case history 'vignettes' within the book which support the themes I have sought to develop. Some of the material draws from ideas developed with others, in particular David Ballantyne, Moira Clark, Uta Jüttner, Adrian Payne and Helen Peck – all members, past or present, of the Cranfield marketing and logistics team.

Finally, grateful thanks are due to Tracy Brawn who cheerfully worked her way through numerous drafts of the manuscript and to Natalie Saunders who created the graphics.

Martin Christopher

CHAPTER 1

The new market place

A new market place is emerging in many Western economies – one that is characterized by sophisticated and demanding customers and consumers and where the competitive environment is more volatile and less predictable. In these conditions the classic marketing reliance on the '4 Ps' of product, price, promotion and place is no longer sufficient to achieve market leadership. Instead, winning companies are those that can speed up the rate of innovation, bring new products and services to the market place faster, replenish demand with shorter lead-times and greater reliability – in short these companies are more responsive. Creating the responsive organization has to be the main priority of management in any business and to achieve this will require a much greater focus on the *processes* through which demand is met. This is the arena of marketing logistics – the critical interface between the market place and the organization seeking to satisfy customer requirements.

In recent years there has been a growing questioning of the effectiveness of marketing as it has conventionally been practised. Whilst the basic principles of marketing still hold – that is the identification of customer needs and the satisfaction of them at a profit to the supplier – there is some doubt as to whether the focus of 'traditional' marketing upon branding and positioning is still appropriate. In this classic model the routes to competitive advantage have typically been based upon strong brands, corporate images, media advertising and, in some cases, price. These are the classic components of conventional marketing strategies. In today's turbulent market place however, it is no longer sufficient to have attractive products, competitively priced and creatively advertised. There has been a growing tendency for customers to want more – specifically to require even higher levels of service.

"In today's turbulent market place it is no longer sufficient to have attractive products, competitively priced and creatively advertised"

Customer service is the new competitive battleground. It can provide a significant opportunity to differentiate an otherwise standard product and an opportunity to tailor the company's offering to meet specific customer requirements.

This trend towards the *service-sensitive* customer is as apparent in industrial markets as it is in consumer markets. Hence companies supplying the car industry, for example, must be capable of providing just-in-time deliveries direct to the assembly line; similarly a food manufacturer supplying a large supermarket chain must have an equivalent logistics capability, enabling it to keep the retail shelf filled whilst minimizing the amount of inventory in the system. The evidence from across a range of markets suggests that the critical determinant of whether orders are won or lost, and hence the basis for becoming a preferred supplier, is customer service. Time has become a far more critical element in the competitive process. Customers in every market want ever shorter lead-times; product availability will overcome brand or supplier loyalty – meaning that if the customer's preferred brand is not available and a substitute is, then the likelihood is a lost sale.

The changing marketing environment

It has to be recognized that there have been some radical changes in the marketing environment since marketing first came to prominence in the early 1960s. Organizations that had even the most rudimentary understanding of the marketing concept were able to reap the harvest of fast-growing markets comprising customers who had money to spend. In such conditions it was easy to believe that the company's marketing effort was the main driver of this success. In reality that success was due as much to the fact that the business was being carried along with the tidal wave of market growth.

"The most significant change to impact Western companies has been the maturing of the markets in which they compete"

The most significant change to impact Western companies has been the maturing of the markets in which they compete. Mature markets have certain characteristics that mark them out as being significantly different from growth markets. Chief amongst the characteristics of mature markets are:

- Sophisticated and experienced customers
- Reduced cost effectiveness of advertising
- Perceived equality of product functionality
- Price competition.

(i) Customer sophistication

In the majority of Western economies, today's customer and consumer has seen it all, they have been there and 'bought the T-shirt'. In industrial markets, as well as fast-moving consumer goods markets, the supplier is now faced with a buyer who is much more demanding and less easily persuaded by marketing 'hype'. One consequence of this change is the gradual decline in brand loyalty in many markets. Brand *loyalty* has been replaced by brand *preference*. What this means is that the buyer may prefer to buy a particular product from a particular supplier for a variety of reasons, e.g. physical characteristics, attributes, convenience, etc. However, this is not the same as loyalty. If, for example, a product is out of stock on the shelf, is the shopper willing to take another brand? Often they are. Or if an original equipment manufacturer finds that delivery lead-times from one supplier are not as reliable as those provided by a competitor, then the likelihood is that the business will switch. Buyers in industrial markets are increasingly subjecting suppliers to rigorous 'vendor appraisals' and will switch suppliers if performance fails to meet their requirements – knowing that a product of equivalent technical quality is available from alternative sources.

Fairy casts a spell over own-label

Judging by the response to a 7p price cut on a boring old bottle of washing-up liquid, an observer from Mars would think the British business community was taking leave of its senses. When Procter & Gamble decided to reduce the price of Fairy Liquid from 79p to 72p, the stock market sent share prices of its main rival, Unilever, and the UK's biggest supplier of own-label products, McBride, into a spin. Subsequent reports that P&G is slicing its vast advertising budget to pay for a price war against own-label brands widened the tizzy to include media magnates.

But they can relax – for the moment. P&G is not becoming a discounter. While it was cutting Fairy's price, it was also pushing up the prices of other products such as Lenor fabric conditioner and its big-box washing powders. Nor is P&G cutting ad spends. What it is doing is trying to reduce the proportion of income it spends on marketing while still spending more as sales increase. 'It's all about getting smarter and increasing efficiency,' says Dick Johnson, P&G's vice-president of corporate affairs.

A storm in a washing-up bowl, then? No. P&G's rivals and agencies daren't relax for too long. The Fairy initiative is just one of many now emerging from its formidable marketing machine. When combined they could rewrite the rules of grocery marketing.

P&G is, for example, planning to transform the way it deploys its £5 billion global marketing budget. The changes kick in next year, but already, says Mr Johnson, 'we target our advertising much better than we used to, and we schedule it much more effectively'. And, he adds: 'We have got to look at ways other than television. We are spending more and more of our money on direct marketing.'

Meanwhile, P&G is leading the grocery industry in a series of initiatives designed to get manufacturers and retailers working more closely together. The marketing powerhouse is re-examining every step in the distribution chain, from deciding what new products get launched and how, to how goods are transported, to what gets displayed on the shelves, at what price, with what sort of promotion.

At the same time, P&G is introducing a strategy of low pricing in areas where it doesn't like the way the market is going, especially if own-brands are booming.

Take washing-up liquids. Over the past two years, Fairy has been embroiled in a typical grocery marketing bloodbath. With nearly 50 per cent of the market, Fairy's rivals (including own-label) have gone all out to attack it, creating new 'flavours' and luring Fairy buyers away with a constant cycle of 'buy-one-get-one-free' style promotions.

Meanwhile the supermarkets have opened up a price gap. According to Nielsen, the market researchers, over the past two years brand manufacturers have pushed up their average price from £1.22 per kg to £1.31. But the supermarkets have driven down the average price of their own-label liquids from 83p per kg to 76p per kg. Two years ago, brands were a hefty 49 per cent more expensive than own-label. Today they are 72 per cent more so. In a static market, own-label volume sales have soared 35 per cent while brand sales are down 8 per cent.

Now P&G has fired a broadside against such marketing tactics. Proliferating the number of non-essential varieties creates confusion for consumers, not choice, it says. Constant promotional activity creates cost and complexity in the grocery distribution chain, and worse, it sows distrust and confusion in consumers' minds, training them to become bargain hunters, buying by price, not by brand.

Hence the Fairy price cut. By ploughing funds earmarked for promotions straight into consistently lower prices, P&G hopes to force competitors to do the same. 'You've got to reward your loyal consumers consistently and not unglue them continually by short-term promotional offers,' says John Millen, P&G's UK vice-president for sales.

(ii) Decline in the impact of advertising

It has been suggested by some commentators that, with the decline of the mass-market and the consequent fragmentation of markets into smaller segments, conventional media-based advertising, particularly TV, is costing more and more to deliver the requisite ratings. This is causing a re-think in many organizations as to how they allocate their marketing budget. For example, it is reported that in the UK Heinz is planning to divert most of its marketing communications budget from TV and apply it instead to direct marketing. Procter & Gamble have also embarked upon a strategy of reducing their TV media spend and are focusing instead on 'everyday low prices'.

In consumer marketing particularly, advertising has long been seen as a powerful means of building significant differential advantage. Whilst there can be no question that a strong media presence provides a foundation for market place success, it seems that more and more buying decisions are taken at the point of purchase, suggesting that on-the-shelf presence is as important as media presence.

"more and more buying decisions are taken at the point of purchase"

(iii) Perceived product equality

Mature markets exhibit similar characteristics to commodity markets in that customers perceive little difference between competing offers. In such conditions, as we have suggested, if the preferred brand is not available, customers will willingly accept a substitute. Even product/markets with high rates of innovation do not seem immune from this tendency to 'commoditization'. Take, for example, the personal computer market, where clones and 'me-toos' now account for significant market shares.

The commoditization of the computer industry

In the early 1960s IBM controlled 70 per cent of the computer market through its disparate range of incompatible computers. Periodically, customers – large corporations, governmental or institutional bodies, who leased rather than bought the colossally expensive computers – would upgrade or replace the equipment. The change inevitably subjected the customer to the expense of rewriting programs, regardless of whether the replacement machine was provided by IBM or a competitor. In 1964, wishing to reduce the risk of customer defections at this critical juncture, IBM standardized its programming thus providing a real incentive for customers to stay with 'Big Blue'. In doing so IBM created an enduring industry standard, and a reputation for marketing prowess. The new standard effectively gave IBM control of the wider computing environment, and a brand that spelled service, safety and continuity in an uncertain world.

Information systems were, despite their expense, horribly unreliable. Buying the wrong system could be the kiss of death to a corporate career, but no-one, it was said, was ever sacked for buying IBM. If an IBM system went wrong, then at least 'Big Blue' had the size and staying power to be around to help.

Few competitors could compete directly with the industry giant, but many smaller players, including minicomputer makers Digital Equipment Corporation and Hewlett Packard, found unexploited niches where IBM had not yet set a standard. Meanwhile other smaller entrepreneurial outfits enjoyed symbiotic relationships with Big Blue, developing programs and peripherals which complemented and enhanced IBM's massively profitable product range.

Towards the end of the 1970s a new wave of competitors sprang up, drawn in by IBM's fat margins. The newcomers, led by the Amdahl Corporation, built and attempted to market whole computers that were IBM-compatible, but bigger, faster, and above all cheaper than IBM's own machines. In 1979, IBM was forced to cut prices, suffering its first earnings drop in 28 years. The Amdahl Corporation – no longer able to undercut IBM to a degree that was sufficient to overcome the fear and perceived risk of a non-IBM purchase – was squeezed to the brink of oblivion. Scorched by the incident, IBM launched itself, and the industry as a whole, with quickened pace on a path towards the development of new basic technologies that would provide greater computing power at lower cost. In doing so the industry was adhering to the maxim of Moore's law, a phenomenon identified in 1965 by Gordon Moore, a founder of the semiconductor manufacturer, Intel Corporation. Moore postulated that measured against price, the performance of semiconductor technology doubles every 18 months.

Slimmer margins demanded higher volumes, so speed of development became more important than ever. IBM gradually moved to wider market coverage, competing head-on in the minicomputer sector, and following others into the growing microcomputer market. But the falling price of computing power had already conjured up a new breed of competitor, the personal computer makers. IBM hesitated at first but then, in August 1981, plunged into this turbulent new segment with the launch of its personal computer – the 'PC'.

The PC was the first computer IBM had produced, the components of which were largely supplied by outsiders. These outsourced components included the core microprocessors and the operating system that harness their power. IBM had the capabilities to deliver both, but hurrying to get the PC to market, chose instead to outsource both through non-exclusive agreements. The microprocessors came from Intel, and the operating system from an obscure software producer called Microsoft. IBM simply brought the parties together, and then using its legendary marketing capabilities and powerful brand, marketed the product.

The PC was technologically unremarkable but, bearing the IBM logo, it was an immediate success. By 1984, Big Blue held 34 per cent of the exploding personal computer market, and 60-70 per cent of the corporate segment. Analysts predicted that the corporate segment would provide the greatest growth in forthcoming years, both in terms of hardware sales and service contracts. IBM was riding higher than ever, turning in record profit growth, even by its own exceptional standards. In the eyes of thousands of nervous corporate buyers, the IBM logo on the outside of the PC did more than inspire confidence in IBM's own product, it legitimized the entire personal computer sector.

IBM had originally envisaged that most personal computers would be linked up to its still relatively high-margin mainframes, spurring demand for the latter. It realized, too late, that the cheap and increasingly versatile personal computers were gnawing away at its high-end business. Worse still, IBM had maintained its value-added service strategy for mainframes, but opted to distribute its PCs through third-party retailers, removing the opportunity to add service value to its technologically undifferentiated product. Big Blue had left the door wide open for low-cost clones using cheaper distribution and direct service provision to undercut the PC. By 1990 hundreds of IBM-clone makers had sprung up to fill the value vacuum, many of them aided and abetted by Microsoft and Intel.

IBM's brand had fostered Microsoft and speeded the growth of Intel, providing a market for their products and imbuing them with the credibility of their host. With their credibility established, two vital value-added suppliers actively encouraged entrepreneurial new personal computer makers to adopt the latest Microsoft/Intel architectures, undercutting, outpacing, and outperforming IBM. The clone manufacturers found a ready market for their products. Recession had made corporate buyers more value conscious and far more willing to shop around. As computing became cheaper, buying decisions were decentralized and pushed down the organization. Younger corporate buyers with no manufacturer loyalties increasingly viewed hardware as a commodity. The real value lay in services, software and the new applications created by better basic technology.

By the early 1990s, it was Microsoft and Intel, not IBM, that dictated the nature and velocity of competition within the computer industry. Worldwide, 80 per cent of personal computers sold in 1995 carried the 'Wintel' combination of Microsoft's Windows software and Intel's Pentium chips. The 'commoditization' of the computer industry had finally happened.

Inevitably, the commoditization of markets means that companies will need to increase the rate of innovation. Recognizing that inevitably successful products and technologies will be imitated, leading companies invest more in R&D and in particular focus on reducing time-to-market. One reason for the undoubted success of 3M, for example, has been its continued emphasis on seeking to create the conditions that encourage innovation and its attention to managing the processes that bring that innovation to the market.

"the commoditization of markets means that companies will need to increase the rate of innovation"

(iv) Price competition

Almost by definition the combined effect of the previous three factors is a downward pressure on price. As a result, there is a temptation to seek to achieve tactical gains in sales volume through discounting in one form or another which is compounded by the continuing demands for price reductions by powerful customers. Paradoxically, the more that organizations compete on price, the more they reinforce the customers' view that they are indeed commodity suppliers.

Later in this book we will argue that because price and value are so closely linked in the customer's mind, the only option to avoid price competition is to focus on enhancing customer value. The 1990s have been labelled the 'value decade' and this is manifested in a reluctance of customers to pay more unless they believe they are getting more. The case of Marlboro cigarettes in the USA exemplifies the reality of the value decade. April 2, 1993 was termed 'Marlboro Friday' on Wall Street, New York, because of major falls in the share prices of most branded goods companies. The trigger for this collapse had been the decision by Philip Morris to cut the price of its Marlboro cigarettes by 20 per cent or 40 cents a pack in order to counter competition from low price own-label products. The reason suggested by commentators for the fall in the share price of branded goods companies was that the Marlboro episode signalled the beginning of a revolt by customers who were starting to question the worth of paying significantly more for branded products which were no longer seen as delivering a commensurate amount of added value.

"the only option to avoid price competition is to focus on enhancing customer value"

Concentration of buying power

A further significant difference in today's marketing environment, compared to the past, is the continuing concentration of buying power in many markets. Market concentration has occurred as organizations merge or grow through take-overs, and as the inevitable result of a competitive process that leads to the 'survival of the fittest'.

This process of concentration seems to be present in just about every industry. The grocery retail market is a very visible example. Figure 1.1 shows the percentage of the total market in Western European economies accounted for by the top five retailers in those countries.

In those same markets, there are beginning to emerge pan-European buying groups which will add to the concentration effect. These groups seek to use their combined buying power to gain better prices than they might be able to achieve by acting alone.

"A further significant difference in today's marketing environment is the continuing concentration of buying power in many markets"

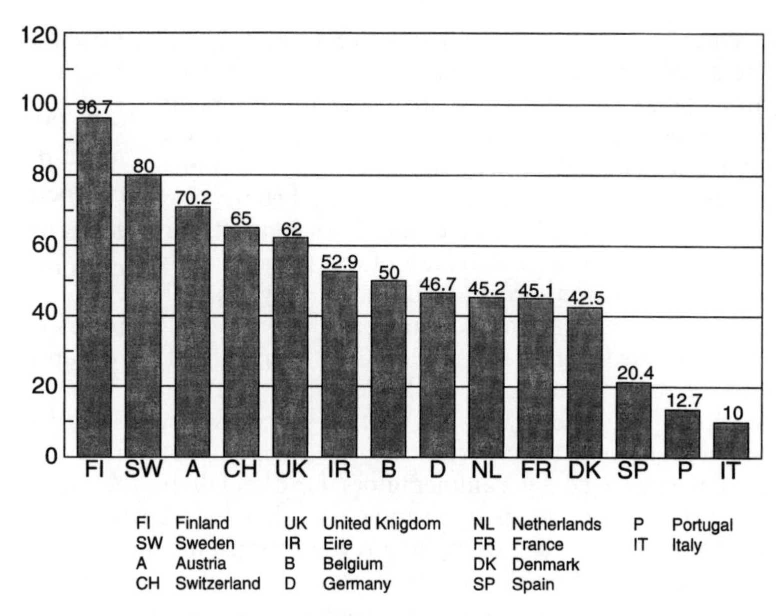

Figure 1.1 Market share of top five retailers. *Source*: AIM

The process of concentration in other industries in Western Europe has been further accelerated through European economic integration. Previously, countries had tended to develop their own industrial base independently from their neighbours, but now that the barriers to trade have mostly been removed there exists significant over-capacity in many industries. If a comparison were to be made between the United States and the countries of the European Union – in total the size of their populations are roughly similar – then it will be found that in many cases in comparable industries there tend to be more players in Europe than in the States. A good example is provided by the turbine generator industry where there are ten companies competing in that market in Europe compared to only two in the United States.

At the same time that customers are growing in purchasing power so also are they seeking to do business with fewer suppliers. Many companies have active programmes of supplier rationalization underway. For example, Rank Xerox's European manufacturing operations at the start of the 1990s were receiving products and services from over 5000 suppliers; at the end of the decade it will be closer to 300. To become a preferred supplier in this new competitive environment clearly demands competencies and capabilities that go beyond the traditional '4 Ps' marketing mix.

A shrinking supply of suppliers

American auto makers will rely on fewer parts suppliers in 1996. Ford Motor Co., for example, has reduced its stable from 10,000 to 2300 – and aims for 1150 by the decade's end. At the same time, Detroit has suppliers building a larger percentage of the content of its cars than ever.

What gives? The consolidation is driven by auto makers who lean on suppliers to provide entire systems for vehicles – an entire dashboard, for instance, instead of just the ashtray that goes into it. Detroit is handing off more development responsibility to suppliers, too. This favours those companies with plentiful capacity, capital and skills. Smaller players must merge or lose the business. Some become second or third tier suppliers to the remaining giants. The Big Three want global supply networks. A supplier who aspires to US business in 1996 may have to be able to deliver the same parts to factories in Germany or Brazil.

Among those that analysts say may grow by acquisition in 1996: Borg-Warner Automotive, Dana and Lear Seating. Says TRW Inc. Chairman Joseph T. Gorman: 'There will continue to be massive (supplier) consolidation as markets that were once national or regional become global.'

The fragmentation of consumer markets

Paradoxically, whilst buying power in business-to-business markets is tending to concentrate, in consumer markets the trend has been to fragmentation. By fragmentation is meant a transition from the old idea of a uniform, homogeneous, 'mass-market' to much smaller segments where consumers seek individual solutions to their buying needs. The emerging idea of 'micro-marketing' is an attempt to focus marketing strategies upon ever smaller groupings of customers. For example, food retailers are now creating merchandising strategies for individual stores based upon the analysis of local geo-demographic data and sales patterns from scanner data. In a different market, Dell Computers will configure a PC from a

"'micro-marketing' is an attempt to focus marketing strategies upon ever smaller groupings of customers"

range of options and still have the equipment delivered direct to the customer.

The aim of micro-marketing is to get as close as possible to the ultimate 'segment of one' whereby tailored solutions for individual customers are put together. Clearly to get anywhere close to this requires a significant element of flexibility and ever higher levels of responsiveness on the part of the supplier.

In the fragmented market place the conventional tools of mass-marketing no longer have the same effect. National advertising campaigns through the mass media, for example, may no longer be the most cost-effective way of communicating with these micro-markets. At the same time there is evidence that the more sophisticated consumer is influenced less by traditional advertising and that more purchase decisions are actually made at the point of sale.

However, whilst mass media communication may no longer be cost-effective in reaching micro-markets, the new techniques of 'database marketing' (DBM) can assist in understanding and communicating with customers who have specific characteristics and attributes. Using data from a variety of sources and powerful computing technology it is possible to zero in on relatively small groups of customers with similar profiles. This enables a highly targeted approach to marketing communications to be effected.

Making use of computerized customer information files which are constructed on a 'relational' basis (i.e. different elements of information can be brought together from separate files) enables the marketer to target more precisely the message to the individual customer or prospective customer.

It is not just computer technology that has made DBM a reality, it is also the rapid growth in the availability of detailed information on individual customers in many markets. A major spur to the use of DBM in consumer markets particularly has come through the rapidly developing field of *geo-demographics.*

Geo-demographics is the generic term applied to the construction of relational databases which draw together data on demographic variables (e.g. age, sex, location), socio-economic variables (e.g. occupation, income), purchase behaviour, lifestyle information and indeed any data that might usefully describe the characteristics of an individual customer.

Much of this information is available through sources such as the census of population, electoral rolls, Target Group Index (TGI), National Shoppers' Survey (NSS), credit card purchase data and so on, all of which can be related to post code areas and, in some cases, to individuals.

Commercially available geo-demographic databases such as ACORN, PINPOINT and MOSAIC can greatly assist marketing to target far more precisely the appropriate audience. It is now possible to identify with a high level of accuracy the characteristics of every one of the UK's fifteen million postcodes – each with a maximum of about 15 addresses.

One of the major opportunities that DBM provides is the facility to profile the organization's existing customer base and then to seek other potential customers with similar profiles. Similarly the increasingly detailed information on individuals' purchase behaviour that is now available makes it much easier to target them with appropriate communications for products or services.

DBM also facilitates a much greater degree of personalization of customer contact. Direct mail can be made more specific to the recipient. Catalogues, newsletters – even magazines – can be tailored to the known interests and preferences of the individual. One company in the USA, Donnelly, provides a specialized printing service so that many different versions of a single magazine can be printed with tailored editorial and advertising content to small groups of subscribers. One magazine, *Farm Journal*, is printed in 8000 different editions, each one of which going to a specific segment of readers, according to their demographic profile, farm size, type of crop or livestock, and so on.

Retailers have been amongst the first to recognize the marketing opportunities for building customer loyalty provided by DBM. Customers are encouraged to register for 'frequent shopper' programmes and to benefit from discounts and special promotions if they present their card at the check-out counter when making their purchases. As a result the customer's precise purchase history can be recorded along with their demographic profile, lifestyle and other details. This enables tailored promotions to be offered, cross selling to be facilitated and, importantly, the merchandise mix in that store to be matched more precisely to the customers' requirements. As we have already noted, many retail chains are developing specific merchandise and marketing strategies for individual stores so that a store patronized by shoppers with particular demographic profiles and known purchasing preferences will carry a mix of products appropriate to the customer base.

The use of DBM is spreading widely in the service industries. Frequent flyer schemes and hotel club schemes have been around for some time, but now their potential is being more fully utilized. Thus not only is the individual's purchase behaviour known, but this can be correlated with the background information previously collected on that individual.

Tesco Clubcard

On 13 February 1995, grocery multiple Tesco launched 'Clubcard', the UK's first national supermarket loyalty scheme. A spokesman for Tesco explained that the principal objective of the scheme was not to lure shoppers away from competitors' stores. Clubcard was, he claimed, 'a way of saying thank you' to existing customers. He went on to add that Tesco was aiming to recreate the kind of relationship that had existed between local shops and their customers 50 years ago.

Membership of the Clubcard scheme is open to all Tesco customers, through any of its 519 stores. Cards are issued on application. The customer then presents the magnetic stripe card at the checkout, where it is swiped through existing credit card reading equipment. Details of the purchases are recorded, with Clubcard points automatically awarded for every £5 spent in the store, over a minimum of £10 per visit. At the end of each quarter, points are added up, and (provided the customer has accumulated a minimum of 50 points) money-off vouchers are mailed to the customers' homes, to be redeemed against future spending. The scheme will allow customers to claim a 1 per cent discount on their annual shopping bills.

The costs of running the Clubcard scheme are considerable. In addition to the 1 per cent discount to shoppers, Tesco anticipated that the start-up costs alone were likely to be in the region of £5m. But the company is convinced that this is money well spent. During pre-launch trials at 14 stores, over 250,000 Clubcards were issued, representing an uptake at the sites involved of between 70–80 per cent. During the trials, high spending customers were identified and given special treatment, including invitations to 'meet the staff' cheese and wine evenings at their local stores. The customers responded favourably to the scheme and appeared to enjoy the events.

Speculation was rife that within a matter of weeks, other leading supermarket chains would be forced to follow with their own national loyalty schemes. In a statement to the press, David Sainsbury, chairman of market leader J. Sainsbury, dismissed the scheme as a 'Green Shield Stamp way of offering value'. In his opinion 'the scheme will cost at least £10m to administer. That's wasted money which brings no benefits at all to customers. We have no plans at all to go down that route.' But the Green Shield Stamp analogy missed an important point. Tesco was looking for more than a temporary gain in market share from its £5m investment. It was buying a wealth of self-renewing information about its current customer base.

Operational benefits – such as refined stock selection, display and staffing levels – can be derived from the data, and should not be overlooked, but the primary purpose of the data gathering is to facilitate micro-marketing activities. The stream of customer purchase data – what they purchase, how much they spend, when, and how often – reveals a great deal about the lifestyles of shoppers themselves. From this data Tesco can segment its customer base according to real purchase behaviour rather than a version of purchase behaviour based on demographic or socioeconomic stereotypes. The data could be used to build loyalty through tailored, value-based offers, mailed to homes of specific groups of customers. The attractiveness or value of the offer to the customers concerned can be measured by the take-up rate.

By the end of March 1995, over 5 million people had joined the clubcard scheme and Tesco recorded a 7 per cent like-for-like increase in sales. According to independent research, Tesco's sales had (for the first time) surged ahead of Sainsbury to become Britain's leading retailer of packaged goods. Clubcard had delivered a 2 per cent increase in Tesco's market share, with a 1 per cent increase in household penetration – meaning that an additional 200,000 households had come to shop at Tesco's stores. Over a third of the gains were reported to have been at Sainsbury's expense. Tesco endeavoured to play down reports of market-share gains, saying that it is the fact that it is pleasing the customer that really counts. In the meantime it continued to recruit Clubcard members and proceeded to build its formidable database of customer buying behaviour.

Relationships can thus be enhanced because it becomes possible to customize the service, for example seating and food preferences on an airline or room preferences in an hotel can be easily catered for.

Fast-moving consumer goods (FMCG) companies are increasingly able to pinpoint likely targets for their products through the use of DBM but, more importantly, they can use it to strengthen relationships with key customers by designing promotions and incentives that will bind customers more closely to the company. For example, data through surveys such as the National Shoppers' Survey (NSS) is available on over three million individual customers in the UK, enabling marketers to target heavy users in their product category, or to select users of competitive products for targeted promotions.

In consumer durables more and more car companies are using DBM to improve customer retention rates. Saab, for example, collect a great deal of detail on each of their customers at the time they buy a car (then they up-date it every six months). Using this information, Saab can design appropriate joint promotions with other companies with a high level of potential appeal to Saab customers – recent examples include Bang & Olufsen and Laurent Perrier champagne. As the time approaches when existing customers are likely to be in the market for a new car, then an individually focused marketing programme begins. Clearly if the company knows who the key prospects are, it can afford to spend a lot more on sales and marketing per individual and that sales and marketing effort will be much more effective because it is specific to an individual.

Many business-to-business marketing companies have yet to realize the opportunity that DBM presents. It is often the case that they do not realize the amount of data that exists about their clients or potential clients. Some of the leaders in the use of DBM began by widening the scope of their existing customer enquiry systems. Thus CSX, a major North American transport company, tracks every one of its customers' shipments, firstly so that they can provide status reports to customers on the location of a particular shipment, but secondly so that it can tailor its services more precisely to individual customer requirements.

"Database marketing is transforming the ways in which fragmented markets can be addressed"

Database marketing is transforming the ways in which fragmented markets can be addressed and individualized communications delivered. Combine this with flexibility of response in terms of the design and delivery of products or services and a significant competitive opportunity emerges.

The service sensitive customer

It has now become an accepted fact of commercial life that customer service is a critical determinant in winning and keeping customers. Today's customer in virtually every market is demanding ever-higher levels of performance from suppliers, particularly in respect to delivery service. In many organizations the focus upon inventory reduction has caused them to look closely at the quality of the in-bound delivery service they receive from suppliers. At the other end of the marketing channel, consumers have become equally demanding in their service requirements. In the era of fast food and convenience stores, there is less willingness to wait. As a result, on-the-shelf availability will often overcome brand preference as we have already observed.

"Today's customer in virtually every market is demanding ever-higher levels of performance from suppliers"

The challenge to the organization that aspires to be a leader in service performance is to recognize the service requirements of the different segments that it services and to re-structure its logistics processes around the achievement of those service requirements.

Organizations in virtually every market sector have come to recognize that differentiation through superior customer service offers an opportunity to avoid price competition. Whilst there will always be 'price buyers' in any market there are also large numbers of service sensitive customers. The success of Marks & Spencer in selling, at relatively high prices, oven-ready gourmet-style meals demonstrates that there are significant numbers of customers who are 'time sensitive' rather than 'price sensitive'. In a rather different market Electrocomponents, an electronic parts distributor, has been able to maintain above-average margins as a result of above-average service (see case study).

Using service to sell

Swift delivery of essential components is the secret of Electrocomponents' success. It sells over 59,000 electronic, electrical and mechanical components and has recently added health and safety devices used in the workplace. In most cases the items are distress purchases. Buyers want a vital part urgently to mend a machine. At times like this, price comes way down the list of priorities for customers. Much more important is speed of delivery, reliability of product and certainty of supply. Electrocomponents guarantees delivery within two hours of an order in some cases and customers pay a premium to get products quickly.

This helps Electrocomponents to maintain high margins. In the six months to September they were a healthy 15.7 per cent.

Investors' Chronicle, 24 November 1995

The sources of marketing advantage

In the new competitive environment, it is increasingly evident that successful marketing strategies are based upon an amalgam of three critical elements: the creation of a *consumer franchise* whereby end-users are attracted to the product/service in question because they perceive a superior offer; a strong *customer franchise* where intermediaries want to do business with us because of a tangible economic benefit and, third, an underpinning *supply chain effectiveness* that delivers superior service at less cost. Figure 1.2 summarizes the three sources of competitive advantage.

Each of the three dimensions requires a clearly defined strategy, but developed as part of an integrative package to deliver superior value to customers and consumers alike.

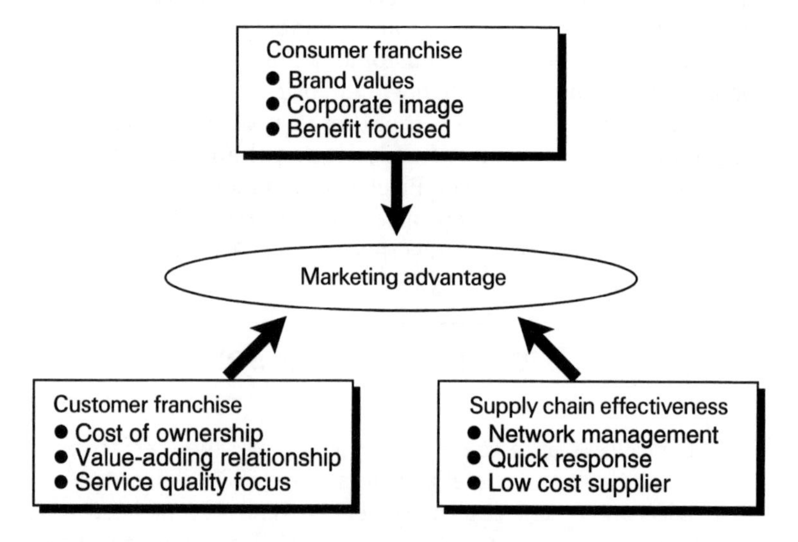

Figure 1.2 The sources of marketing advantage

(i) The consumer franchise

Whilst brand loyalty may no longer be as strong as it once was, the need to build a 'contract' with the end-user is still a vital pre-requisite for marketing advantage. Brand value is still a critical element in many purchase decisions although it seems that there has been a return to a concept of value based upon tradi-

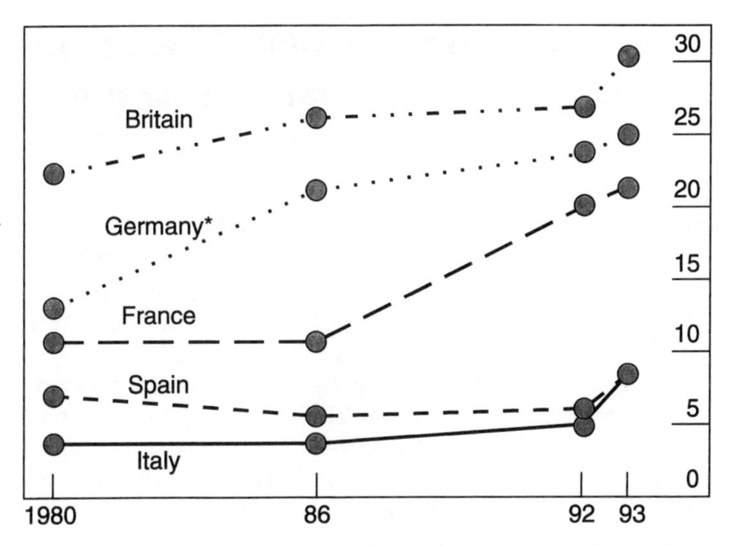

Figure 1.3 Own label market share (percentage). *Source*: Boston Consulting Group. *Figures do not include Aldi

tional tangible or 'core' benefits rather than the more emotionally-based, intangible benefits that seem to have fixated many marketers in the last quarter-century. Now it seems that consumer loyalty more often is based upon 'hard' rather than 'soft' dimensions. So, value for money, convenience, reliability, safety and functionality become the drivers of product or service choice. We buy a TV set more for its features and the reputation of its manufacturer for reliability than we do for its image, for example. The impact of own-label, retailer-branded products in many categories is further testimony to this development. Coca-Cola, regarded as the world's most recognized brand, has seen its market share in the USA and the UK (and elsewhere too) eroded by own-label products which are seen by customers to deliver better value for money. Figure 1.3 shows the growing penetration of own-label products in major European markets.

What this means for twenty-first-century marketers is that in order to strengthen the consumer franchise, the focus of marketing effort must increasingly be upon delivering 'solutions' which can be translated into hard, tangible benefits for individual consumers. In many cases this will further hasten the transition to 'micro' or 'one-to-one' marketing whereby a greater degree of tailoring/customization of the product offer is achieved.

The Cola wars: own-label takes on the world's most famous brand

The news that Marlboro cigarettes, flagship brand of the American tobacco industry, had bowed to price competition from own-label cigarettes sent a shock wave through corporate America. Nowhere more so than in the headquarters of Coca-Cola, home of the world's most valuable brand. The devaluation of the Marlboro brand was certain to put pressure on the stock of other premium label holders. Within hours of the announcement Coca-Cola executives had devised a two-pronged damage limitation plan for Coke. Retailers would be wooed with detailed explanations of how a premium brand could attract high spending grocery shoppers. Meanwhile presentations to analysts would highlight why Coke was much less vulnerable to own-label competition than Marlboro had been. The latter emphasized that although Coke did command a price premium over own-label products, the price differential was not so large as to sway customers towards lower quality alternatives. They were, therefore, confident that American cola buyers and fellow consumers around the world would stay loyal to the Coca-Cola brand, or at worse, to its perennial rival Pepsi.

The up-beat presentations dismissed retailer own-label cola on the grounds of inferior quality. This has been true in the past, but it brushed aside a recent offensive launched by Canadian producer, the Cott Corporation. Cott had been an obscure Canadian soft-drinks bottler, a family business, whose Quebec plant had for several decades supplied high quality own-label cola to stores in eastern Canada. In 1989 the company's founder, Harry Pencer, moved aside in favour of his son Gerald, who set about transforming Cott into a manufacturer, supplier and distributor of own-label products, and an international player in the soft-drinks business. Under the new management, Cott quickly expanded its activities throughout Canada and into the neighbouring US.

In the US own-label products were still widely perceived as low quality, low margin alternatives, bought by people who were unable to afford 'the real thing'. Coke and Pepsi both responded to Cott's offensive with new advertising campaigns to bolster their brands, stressing the quality and originality of their products. Coke also decided the time was right to reintroduce its classic hour-glass cola bottle. As a result, own-label cola-sales growth was arrested and returned to the pre-Marlboro Friday levels of around 10 per cent.

In the UK however, the retail terrain is markedly different. The grocery market is dominated by a handful of sophisticated retailers who long ago dispelled any 'cheap and nasty' connotations associated with own-label. Thus extensive ranges of high quality own-label products were offered – many of them supplied by manufacturers of leading brands. Premium label cola was one of the few products that British supermarkets had hitherto been unable to match. Consequently, only 1 per cent of UK cola sales were retailers' own-label.

The situation changed dramatically in November 1993, when Cott deployed a single employee, Simon Lester, to establish a soft-drinks beachhead in Europe. Three months later, J. Sainsbury, one of the UK's leading supermarkets launched 'Sainsbury's Classic Cola', a premium quality cola produced by Cott, attractively packaged to be directly competitive with regular brands. The product was an instant success, immediately becoming the store's best selling cola. Safeway, Britain's third largest supermarket, followed suit with 'Safeway Select Cola'. Meanwhile, music-to-airlines entrepreneur Richard Branson, launched 'Virgin Cola' through a joint venture between Cott and the Virgin Group. Virgin Cola was taken up by several national grocery chains, including Tesco, where it quickly out-sold Coca-Cola. By early 1995 Virgin and the other Cott produced own-label colas had captured 27 per cent of UK supermarket cola sales, boosting sales for the sector and cutting Coke's share from 44 to 32 per cent.

Coca-Cola fought back to protect its remaining market share with price cuts, increased advertising spend and the appointment of a new advertising agency to handle its European account. Nevertheless, by July 1995 Cott had become the world's largest supplier of own-label soft drinks, supplying over 100 retail clients in 14 countries on four continents.

(ii) The customer franchise

Because the power of intermediaries has strengthened in many markets, it is of paramount importance to make the customer – not just the consumer – an integral part of marketing strategy. Whether the intermediary be a retailer, a distributor or an original equipment manufacturer (OEM), without their support it is unlikely that even the strongest brand could achieve its full potential.

Not only has the purchasing power of the customer increased as a result of concentration, but, as we suggested earlier, there is a growing trend towards 'single-sourcing' by those customers. In other words, whereas in the past the practice was to spread the total purchase of an item across several suppliers, now the aim is to reduce the size of the supplier base and to seek further cost reductions as a result.

Whilst to many suppliers such developments may be perceived as a threat, to others they present an opportunity. If the supplier can offer a superior value package with a measurable positive economic impact on the customer, then the likelihood is that they will win the business. Today's customer is a more sophisticated buyer, used to working with concepts such as total cost of ownership, life-cycle costing and cost/benefit analysis. Indeed, many customers now actively pursue a 'partnership sourcing' concept whereby they seek to establish long-term relationships with preferred suppliers based upon 'win-win' philosophies.

(iii) Supply chain effectiveness

In the new market place there is a strong case for arguing that individual companies no longer compete with other stand-alone companies, but rather that supply chain now competes against supply chain. The rationale for this viewpoint is based upon the fact that when organizations work independently of their up-stream suppliers and down-stream customers, costs and inefficiencies tend to build up at the interfaces.

"supply chain now competes against supply chain"

The need for co-ordination between partners in the supply chain has increased as the 'network organization' becomes more common. The network organization comprises a complex web of linkages between focused partners each of which adds value through specialization in an activity where it can provide a differential advantage.

A company like Apple Computers for example relies heavily upon other companies to supply components, to manufacture hardware, to create software and to distribute its products around the world. Something like 90 per cent or more of the cost of an Apple computer is going to outside suppliers.

This progress towards the idea of supply chain integration as a source of competitive advantage will gain momentum as the growth of 'time-based competition' accelerates. In markets that are increasingly volatile, responsiveness becomes a critical competitive requirement. Companies like Benetton and The Limited have gained significant advantage through their ability to respond rapidly to fashion changes in the markets that they serve. Through the use of highly co-ordinated logistics and supply chain structures, driven by the real-time capture of sales data, these companies, and others like them, can adapt their product range and their volumes in weeks rather than months.

Formalized supply chain management is increasingly being recognized as a critical determinant of competitive advantage. Because both total costs and customer service are heavily impacted by the structure of the supply chain and the effectiveness of its co-ordination, it is essential that a greater emphasis be placed upon its management.

Later in this book examples will be given of organizations that have significantly enhanced their competitive performance through focusing upon improving both upstream and downstream linkages with their supply chain partners. What will be apparent is that this concept of supply chain integration requires a fundamentally different approach to relationships within the marketing channel. Traditional buyer/supplier relationships, which have tended towards the adversarial, need to be reassessed and be replaced with a philosophy of co-operation and 'win-win' thinking.

Chapter checklist
The new market place: key issues

- The changing nature of the market place
  - Customer and consumer sophistication
  - Erosion of brand loyalty and advertising effectiveness
  - Greater use of tactical pricing

- The growth in customer power
  - Concentration of buyer power
  - Customers rationalizing the supplier base
  - Demise of the mass market

- The focus on 'micro-markets'
  - The advent of database marketing
  - The importance of 'geo-demographics'
  - Better target marketing

- The service-sensitive customer
  - The growing importance of customer service
  - Time-sensitive customers
  - Logistics provides competitive advantage

CHAPTER 2

Building customer relationships

As markets mature and the cost of winning new customers steadily increases, greater emphasis needs to be placed upon retaining existing customers and building the business that is done with them. Market share, which for long was the over-riding goal of many corporations, is being replaced by a focus on customer share. In other works what share of the customer's spend are we getting and what is the quality of that share – meaning how loyal are those customers. Much evidence exists to suggest that retained customers are generally more profitable than new customers and hence the marketing challenge is to find ways of building enduring relationships with customers. Whilst many factors will influence the quality and longevity of a customer relationship, it will usually be the case that superior service performance will be a key determinant of customer retention.

Customer retention strategies

It has been suggested that it costs up to five times as much to win a new customer as it does to retain an existing customer. The costs of capturing market share are not always easy to gauge but there are many companies now who regret earlier strategies that were based upon the blind pursuit of volume. Whilst there is strong evidence for the link between market share and profitability there is equally strong evidence to show that it is the *quality* of that market share that counts. In other words does our customer base comprise, in the main, long-established, loyal customers or is there a high degree of turnover or 'churn'? If the latter is the case then the chances are that we are not as profitable as we might be.

The international consulting company, Bain and Company, have suggested that even a relatively small improvement in the customer retention rate (measured as the percentage of retained business from one period to another) can have a marked impact upon profitability. They suggest that on average, an improvement of five percentage points in customer retention can lead to profit improvements of between 25 per cent and 85 per cent in the net present value of the future flow of earnings.

Why should a retained customer be more profitable than a new one? First, because of the costs of acquiring new business in the first place, it might take time to bring a new customer into profit. Second, the more satisfied the customer is with the relationship the more likely they are to place a bigger proportion of their total purchase with us, even to the extent of 'single sourcing' from us. Third, these retained customers become easier to sell to, with consequent lower costs; also they are more likely to be willing to integrate their systems (e.g. their planning, scheduling and ordering systems) with ours, leading to further cost reductions. In some markets satisfied customers may also refer others to us, leading to a further enhancement of profitability. Finally, Bain and Company suggested that loyal customers were often less price sensitive and would be less inclined to switch suppliers because of price rises.

"Why should a retained customer be more profitable than a new one?"

All of these elements together combine to lead to the conclusion that retained customers generate considerably more profit than new ones. Figure 2.1 summarizes this relationship.

A study in the North American car industry suggested that a satisfied customer is likely to stay with the same supplier for a further 12 years after the first satisfactory purchase and, during that period, will buy four more cars of the same make. It is

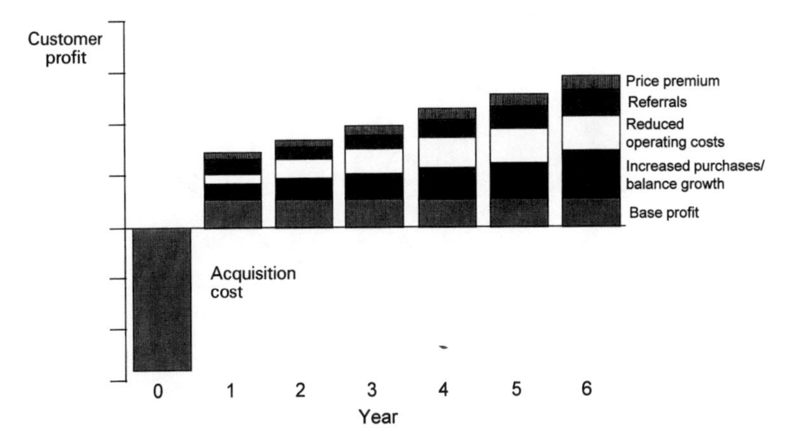

Figure 2.1 Customer profit contribution over time. *Source*: Customer retention model, Bain & Company

estimated that, to a car manufacturer, this level of customer retention is worth US$400 million in new car sales annually.

There is a direct linkage between the customer retention rate and the average lifetime of a customer. For example, if the customer retention rate is 90 per cent per annum (meaning that we lose 10 per cent of our existing customer base each year) then the average customer lifetime will be 10 years. If, on the other hand, we manage to improve the retention rate to 95 per cent per annum (meaning that we lose 5 per cent of our customers each year) then the average customer life will be 20 years. In other words a doubling of the average customer life is achieved for a relatively small improvement in the retention rate. Figure 2.2 illustrates the relationship between the retention rate and the customer lifetime.

"There is a direct linkage between the customer retention rate and the average lifetime of a customer"

An important statistic which is not always measured is the *lifetime value of a customer*. Put very simply this is a measure of the financial worth to the organization of a retained customer. If customers are loyal and continue to spend money with us into the future then clearly their lifetime value is greater than that of a customer who buys only once or twice then switches to another brand or supplier.

Measuring the lifetime value of a customer requires an estimation of the likely cash flow to be provided by that customer if they were to achieve an average loyalty level. In other words if a typical account lasts for ten years then we would need to calculate the net present value of the profits that would flow from

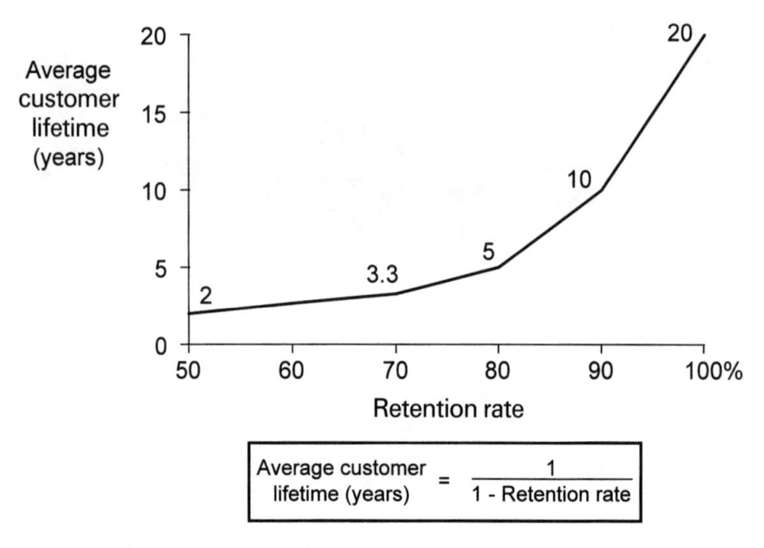

Figure 2.2 Impact of customer retention rate on customer lifetime. *Source*: Bain & Company

that customer over ten years. We are now in a position to calculate the impact that increasing the retention rate of customers would have upon profitability and also what the effect of extending the customer lifetime by a given amount would be. This information provides a good basis for marketing investment decision-making; in other words, how much is it worth spending, either to improve the retention rate or to extend the life of a customer?

Whilst it has long been acknowledged that the fundamental purpose of marketing is the 'getting and keeping of customers', the truth is that more attention has been paid, typically, to the getting of customers rather than the keeping of them. More recently there has emerged a recognition that marketing needs to encompass not only those activities necessary to capture business in the first place, but also to develop processes that will enhance long-term customer loyalty. This viewpoint is the foundation for the development of the concept of *relationship marketing*, at the heart of which lies the proposition that the fundamental purpose of marketing is the creation and development of long-term, profitable relationships with customers.

"more attention has been paid, typically, to the getting of customers rather than the keeping of them"

It should not be thought that relationship marketing is a replacement for marketing as it has been practised to date. Rather it is an augmentation and a re-focusing of the marketing concept with the emphasis placed upon strategies to enhance

Table 2.1 The shift to relationship marketing

Transaction focus	Relationship focus
• orientation to single sales	• orientation to customer retention
• discontinuous customer contact	• continuous customer contact
• focus on product features	• focus on customer value
• short time scale	• long time scale
• little emphasis on customer service	• high customer service emphasis
• limited commitment to meeting customer expectations	• high commitment to meeting customer expectations
• quality is the concern of production staff	• quality is the concern of all staff

customer retention and loyalty. Some of the major differences in emphasis between the traditional approach, which we label 'transactional', and the 'relationship' focus are shown in Table 2.1.

It will be seen from Table 2.1 that the major difference between the relationship focus and the transactional focus is the emphasis upon continuous commitment to meeting the needs of individual customers and that service and quality are particularly stressed. Many marketing practitioners might justifiably protest that they have been practising relationship marketing for years but did not realize it! In truth, however, many others have failed to recognize the importance of customer loyalty as a driver of profitability and hence have tended to concentrate their effort on a single-minded pursuit of market share.

Relationship marketing as a philosophy is concerned with the 'quality' of market share, not just its absolute level, in other words the minimization of customer defections and the building of long-term partnerships with customers who willingly repeat purchase from us.

Relationships as partnerships

The basic philosophy underlying relationship marketing is that the goal of all marketing activity should be the establishment of mutually beneficial partnerships with customers. If customers perceive that there is greater value in staying with a particular supplier than with moving to any other, then clearly they will stay. Hence the challenge to management is to develop marketing strategies that are designed to create enduring customer partnerships.

For example many companies are benefiting from closer relationships with suppliers. What they are discovering is that by working alongside suppliers they can find ways to take costs out of the supply chain by focusing on such things as just-in-time delivery systems, linking ordering procedures through electronic data interchange (EDI) and by eliminating the need for rework by quality improvement programmes. In addition they can build customer value by working together on product improvements and new product development. Indeed some studies suggest that a major source of innovation is from the upstream supplier.

"many companies are benefiting from closer relationships with suppliers"

Emerging from this concept of partnership is the idea of the 'extended supply chain'. Whilst traditionally companies have tended to see their strengths in terms of their own capabilities and resources, this notion of the extended supply chain looks beyond the legal boundaries of the company for new sources of competitive advantage. Supply chain management can thus be defined as the management of upstream and downstream relationships with suppliers, distributors and customers in such a way that greater customer value is achieved at less total cost. The result of a successful supply chain management programme should be enhanced profit for all the partners in the chain.

Managing relationships in the marketing channel

The stronger the relationship with a partner, the greater the barrier to entry that it presents to competitors. For example, suppliers to Marks & Spencer, who have built up exceptionally close linkages over many years, have little to fear from competitors as long as the product and service they provide continues to meet the stringent requirements placed upon them by Marks & Spencer. This is because of the considerable investment made by both parties in product and process development, in linked logistics systems and in continuous improvement programmes.

Getting the prawn sandwich to market

Gunstones Bakery, a subsidiary of the UK food manufacturer Northern Foods, is one of three major suppliers of sandwiches to Marks & Spencer (M&S). Marks & Spencer are Britain's biggest retailers of ready packed sandwiches, selling between one and two million units a week.

Because of the demand for freshness, each sandwich has a maximum shelf life of 48 hours from time of manufacture to point of sale, yet at the same time demand is uncertain since one of the biggest determinants of consumption patterns is the weather! The problem is further compounded by the fact that M&S offer 40 different fillings on eight types of bread. Hence the need for a highly integrated supply chain capable of responding rapidly to ensure that the right product is in the right place at the right time.

Because of the very close working relationship between Gunstones Bakery and Marks & Spencer they are able to achieve an almost seamless flow of sandwiches into M&S's 290 stores across Britain. The process begins when M&S give a provisional order mid-week for the following week. This forecast is based on the previous week's sales by store and is only approximate because of the influence that the weather has upon demand. On Friday a second forecast is issued by M&S which is used by Gunstones to plan their labour requirement for the following week. Gunstones use casual labour with a high degree of flexibility in their hours of work.

The actual firm order only arrives from M&S the previous evening for dispatch the following day. The despatch will take place by 7.30pm on the day of manufacture for delivery, through a number of regional distribution centres, into the stores by 9.00am the following day. So a Wednesday night order is made on Thursday to be in the shops on Friday morning.

M&S reserve the right to change the order up to 8.00am on the morning following its receipt by Gunstones. On occasion they may change the order up to 12 noon, particularly with sudden changes in the weather or if problems arise with M&S's other sandwich suppliers.

Sandwich manufacture at Gunstones begins at 7.00am with the first despatch to the third-party operated chilled distribution centres beginning at 1.30pm and the last at 7.30pm. The sandwiches are packed by Gunstones into trays according to type to enable them to be sorted for store delivery at the distribution centre.

Clearly such a responsive logistics system requires close collaboration, not just between M&S and Gunstones but also between Gunstones and their suppliers. Whilst Gunstones bake their own bread for the sandwiches and can freeze and unfreeze loaves depending upon demand, the biggest challenge is managing the supply of fresh produce and short shelf-life items, e.g. lettuce. In fact Gunstones maintain hourly contact with their suppliers of short shelf-life products and share with them the latest forecasts from M&S.

The key to the effectiveness of the sandwich supply chain is the high level of communication and shared information between all parties in the chain. For example, Gunstones' senior management will be in constant contact with their M&S opposite numbers. Visits to each others premises are made frequently. Gunstones are also seeking constantly to innovate with new sandwich products and manufacturing processes and in so doing will work closely with both M&S marketing personnel as well as the produce suppliers.

The old idea that buyers and sellers should maintain a distance from each other and only concern themselves with 'negotiating a deal' can no longer be sustained. Instead the trend is increasingly towards a much wider, business development focused relationship, where the supplier takes a holistic view of the customer's needs. A good example of this is provided by recent developments in what is sometimes termed 'trade marketing'. Whilst much of the emphasis in traditional marketing has been placed upon end-users to 'pull' the product through the marketing channel, trade marketing is concerned to gain access to the marketing channel and to increase the 'opportunities to buy' experienced by end users. In other words to ensure that maximum shelf space, distribution and availability is achieved. Occasionally these strategies are referred to as 'push' strategies, however such a term implies a production orientation and it is probably better to talk simply in terms of a 'relationship strategy'.

Figure 2.3 highlights the difference between the two approaches. The conventional buyer/supplier interface is a fragile connection, easily broken by competitors, based upon a motivation on the part of the buyer to maximize the margin and, on the part of the seller, a motivation to maximize volume.

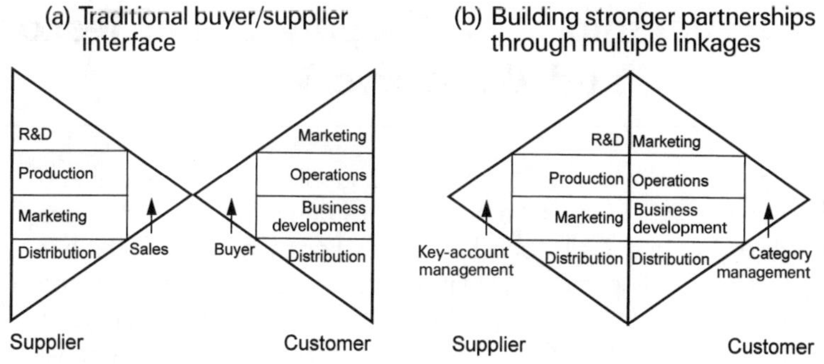

(a) Traditional buyer/supplier interface

R&D
Production
Marketing
Distribution
Sales
Buyer
Marketing
Operations
Business development
Distribution
Supplier
Customer

(b) Building stronger partnerships through multiple linkages

R&D
Production
Marketing
Distribution
Marketing
Operations
Business development
Distribution
Key-account management
Category management
Supplier
Customer

Figure 2.3 The transition to relationship marketing

In the relationship-based approach, the two 'triangles' are inverted to bring about a much stronger interface bond. Now there are multiple points of connection between the vendor and the customer. The objectives of the vendor are to develop the customer's business, to focus on the customer's return on investment and to enhance the customer's own competitive capability. The benefit to the vendor if those objectives are achieved is the likelihood that they will be treated as a preferred supplier. At the same time the costs of serving that customer should be lower as a result of a greater sharing of information, integrated logistics systems and so on.

To achieve such multiple 'connections' between the two parties clearly requires a mutual understanding of the benefits that can be achieved though partnership. In reality it will require a proactive approach from the vendor in which business solutions are presented to the customer, rather than a sales proposition. For example many manufacturers marketing to the retail trade now seek to illustrate the impact of a proposed relationship in terms of return on investment within the category in which the product in question competes. Thus the supplier must be able to demonstrate the impact that the relationship can have upon shelf-space profitability, stock-turn and so on.

This new style partnership approach to channel management challenges much of the conventional thinking about buyer–supplier relationships. It also suggests a more proactive approach to the management of customers, indeed in a growing number of businesses *customer management* has become a key focus of attention.

"This new style partnership approach to channel management challenges much of the conventional thinking about buyer–supplier relationships"

Partnership in the supply chain: Tesco and Birds Eye Wall's

Birds Eye Wall's Ltd is a UK-based supplier of ice creams and other frozen foods, formed in 1981 by the merger of Unilever's Birds Eye and Wall's food businesses. For many years Tesco has been the company's single largest customer, accounting by the late 1980s for over £50 million worth of business per year. However, in 1988 an unscheduled visit from Tesco's commercial director revealed that Birds Eye Wall's (BEW) most important customer was far from satisfied with the service it received from its frozen food supplier.

Tesco was at the time two years into the implementation of a far-reaching quality improvement and cost reduction programme. Hitherto, Tesco had run its retail empire on a supplier stock-push basis, stocking whatever products its suppliers endeavoured to sell, with scant regard for the suppliers' in-store performance. Tesco's suppliers (including BEW) relied on local sales representatives to coax orders from individual store managers. Most of these orders (approximately 70 per cent in BEW's case) would be delivered directly to the stores by the suppliers. Since 1986, Tesco had been working to improve all aspects of its in-store environments, not least product and service quality. In-store performance measures were introduced and, to improve distribution efficiency, Tesco opted to centralize goods flows through its own regional distribution centres. Tesco was moving to take control of replenishment, and investing in improved channels of communication with its suppliers.

The centralization of distribution led to an internal reorganization for Tesco. A 'stock management division' was set up, independent of the related distribution, buying and marketing functions. The new division was given total responsibility for supply chain management, with a remit that encompassed all aspects of stock management including the development of retail systems, and the monitoring and improvement of product service levels. The measures allowed Tesco to bring in continuous replenishment, and to monitor accurately the service performance of its suppliers. Hence the commercial director's unscheduled visit to BEW. Monitoring had revealed that BEW's service level had been as low as 85 per cent for four consecutive weeks, meaning that BEW was consistently meeting only 85 per cent of its orders. This was unacceptably lower than Tesco's 98 per cent target level.

BEW was galvanized into action, rapidly launching 'EXCEL' (a programme of performance improvement measures), and its own internal reorganization. The sales division had been responsible for order taking and distribution, while the marketing section produced sales forecasts, but not stock policy and planning. The latter fell under the auspices of the commercial section. The fragmented organization hampered the flow of information, and consequently product flows. The situation improved significantly with the consolidation of all logistics responsibilities within a single division, which was closely linked to the separately managed manufacturing division. Meanwhile a grass-roots total quality programme was set in motion, establishing internal performance measures throughout the business. Performance was reviewed, by product, on a weekly basis. The results were fed in to create an overall efficiency measure combining stock availability and distribution efficiency (the latter incorporating factory to central distribution point loading and delivery).

Cooperation between BEW and its customers – including Tesco – benefited from broadened communication channels. Where once customer contact had been channelled through a single individual or functional group, multiple points of contact between BEW's functions and the customers' corresponding functions were developed. The benefit was that a disruption to negotiations between BEW and a customer on one issue no longer disrupted on-going communications relating to other matters between the organizations. In 1989 communication between BEW and Tesco took another step forward when BEW began receiving orders from Tesco by EDI. Over the next two years the companies increasingly collaborated over the use of information systems, formally agreeing a joint EDI strategy in 1991. Under the agreement BEW sent Tesco information on product, price, pack size and availability via EDI. In return Tesco used the EDI link to provide its partner with demand and stock forecasting information and electronic payments. Documentation, including orders, confirmations, invoicing and delivery notes would also be exchanged electronically between the two parties.

BEW's performance improved dramatically as a result of the collaboration, rising to 99.5 per cent by 1993. Tesco's stock of BEW's products fell from 3.4 weeks in 1986 to 2.4 week in 1990, and to a single week in 1993, while BEW's own stock halved to 3.5 weeks. Over the same period lead times were reduced from 7 days to 48 hours.

Opting to share forecasting data was a pivotal decision for Tesco. Once committed to the strategy, it began searching for ways to refine the system and maximize the benefits of collaboration. The result was the investment in a store-based ordering system, which allowed store management to abandon time-consuming stock counting reorder systems in favour of minute-by-minute sales data based ordering. By forwarding the sales data on to the suppliers via Tesco's head office, the new system instantly removed artificial fluctuations in demand caused by its predecessor.

Technology provided the tools for the performance gains resulting from the Tesco/BEW partnership, but its continued success arises from the willingness of both parties to regularly review performance levels and continuously work together to tackle new issues and opportunities. Specially appointed teams work closely together to improve forecasting for special promotions, and exchange visits between teams are regularly arranged to improve mutual understanding and cooperation. Meanwhile at the highest levels, the two partners openly discuss further investment in systems development, and define long-term logistics requirements.

Source: Based on Tesco & Birds Eye Wall's, a case study described in *Supplier–Retailer Collaboration in Supply Chain Management*, Project V, The Coca-Cola Retailing Research Group – Europe/GEA Consulenti Associata di gestione aziendale, May 1994, pp 94–96.

Developing a market-driven logistics strategy

Given that customer retention is a key determinant of long-run profitability and that the quality of the relationship with a customer is clearly related to customer retention, what is it that drives the quality of the relationship?

Whilst there will be many influences affecting the quality of a relationship with a customer, it can be argued that a major determinant will be the degree of satisfaction with the service received.

Customer service is a broad concept not easy to define in a single sentence. It encompasses all points of contact between a supplier and a buyer and includes intangible as well as tangible elements. Logistics performance is clearly a critical dimension in achieving customer satisfaction and underpins the model of

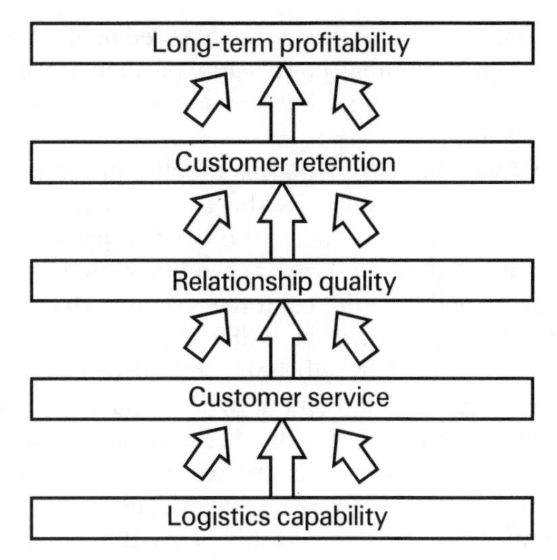

Figure 2.4 Key drivers of long-term profitability

the service-relationship-retention linkage as shown in Figure 2.4.

What this model implies is that successful differentiation through customer service requires more than the obvious focus on 'customer care' and 'putting people first' – important though these are. A critical requirement for an organization seeking to become a service leader in its field is to have a detailed, objective understanding of how customers themselves define service. Once that understanding exists then strategies can be devised and systems developed to meet, or preferably to exceed, customers' expectations.

The argument advanced here is that organizations need to re-define service in terms which have relevance to customers, indeed to use the customers' own definitions of service, and to re-engineer logistics processes so that they are geared to the achievement of those service goals.

"organizations need to re-define service in terms which have relevance to customers"

Traditionally, most measures and standards of customer service are internally focused. In other words they measure dimensions such as stock availability at a stock-keeping unit (SKU) level, inventory cover expressed in terms of number of days sales, percentage of lines available for shipment and so on.

Furthermore the conventional approach to customer service strategy has been based upon the concept of 'trade-offs' to achieve so-called optimal levels of service. In this model all the costs of service provision (e.g. inventory, warehousing, transportation, etc.) are totalled and balanced against the cost of a stock-out. The inevitable conclusion of such an exercise in any market is that the ideal level of service is likely to be less than 100 per cent.

An alternative approach, which is much more in accord with today's focus on total quality, is the idea that the goal of any organization should be to meet 'the service promise' 100 per cent of the time. The *service promise* is a negotiated service package whereby suppliers and customers agree the basis upon which they will trade. It will be a different promise for different customers – not everyone will be promised overnight delivery for example – and the agreement will be based upon a clear knowledge by the supplier of individual customer profitability.

In any purchase situation it is unlikely that there will be more than three or four really critical service issues from a customer's point of view. These we may think of as the 'order winning' criteria and the 'customer retaining' criteria. In other words, these are the elements that the supplying organization must set out to excel upon in each and every customer encounter. Clearly it is essential that the company researches the customer to identify the nature of these criteria and the relative importance attached to them by individual customers.

Not only can this information provide focus for the organization's customer service strategy, but it can provide the basis for a successful market segmentation based upon distinctive service requirements. In other words, instead of offering uniform service packages to all customers, the flexible organization will seek to differentiate the service packages to meet more closely customers' specific requirements.

Researching the customers' service needs

So many companies assume that they understand their customers and so do not recognize the need for detailed, in-depth research amongst existing and potential customers to identify the critical success factors when it comes to winning and keeping business. All definitions of service should be customer-generated and the measurement of service performance should be against customer-relevant metrics.

The following five-step approach is recommended as the basis for establishing a meaningful understanding of customers' service needs and for determining the way those needs may differ by market segment:

Step 1: Define the competitive arena

With whom do we compete in the customer's mind? Often customers compare our performance not so much to other direct 'head-to-head' competitors but rather with other suppliers with whom they do business. Who are the 'best in class' as seen by customers? These are our real competitors.

Step 2: Understand the dimensions of service

Customers are the only ones who can articulate the issues that concern them. Hence the importance of using research to elicit the dimensions of service as seen by customers – rather than our own internal definitions of service. Group interviews or focus groups as well as in-depth interviews can provide the basis for an objective determination of the dimensions of service.

Step 3: Identify the key service issues

Whilst the previous step may have identified multiple issues the key question is: what are the 'order winning' and 'customer keeping' criteria? In other words what are the three or four key dimensions which are critical to the customer's choice of supplier? Research techniques such as trade-off analysis can help quantify the relative importance that customers attach to the different dimensions of service.

Step 4: Recognize the segmentation of the market

It is likely that the research undertaken in Step 3 will reveal that different customers attach different levels of importance to the dimensions of service. In other words not everybody shares the same service priorities. What will often be the case, however, is that clusters or groups of customers will emerge who share similar views on what the key issues are. The clusters may well provide the basis for a re-definition of the market on the basis of service preferences.

Step 5: Measure performance against best-in-class

Using the key service issues, segment by segment, we are now in a position to measure performance against those companies identified by customers in Step 1 as being best-in-class. Such comparisons provide a meaningful benchmark and the basis for the delivery of superior service performance.

Such an approach clearly requires a detailed understanding of customers' needs as well as the value they place upon each element of service. It also requires a level of flexibility throughout the organization to deliver such packages. Adopting this revised model also requires a re-think on how service performance is measured.

"The achievement of the service promise on each and every occasion has been termed 'the perfect order'"

The achievement of the service promise on each and every occasion has been termed 'the perfect order'. The attainment of the perfect order means that each element of the service package has been performed as agreed. One common definition of the perfect order is: 'delivered on-time, complete and error-free'. 'On-time delivery' is measured against the agreed lead-time, 'completeness' is measured by 'order-fill', and 'error-free' includes the avoidance of error in documentation such as invoices as well as other sources of quality failure in the order fulfilment process.

This is quite a challenging measure for even the best run organizations. It must be realized that the overall level of service performance during a period is determined by the *combined* effect of each separate element of the perfect order. Hence performance levels on each element should be multiplied together to provide the real level of service achievement. Thus in the case above:

$$\text{Perfect order achievement} = \% \text{ on-time} \times \% \text{ complete} \times \% \text{ error free}$$

So, for example, if during the past 12 months the actual performance in meeting one customer's requirement was as follows:

90% on-time delivery

80% order-fill

70% error and damage free

then the actual service performance in terms of perfect order achievement would be 90% × 80% × 70% which is approximately 50%!

Creating a customer service index

Using the three or four critical service elements – which may differ by customer or market segment or distribution channel – a continuous monitoring process should be established based around the concept of 'the perfect order'. The perfect order is achieved when all the critical service goals are met to the customer's satisfaction.

For the purpose of illustration the three critical elements identified are:

- On-time delivery
- Order completeness
- Error and damage free

Each of the three elements needs to be carefully defined and accurately measured. The following definitions are proposed:

1: On-time delivery

Number of deliveries in a period that meet the customer's original request divided by the total number of orders received.

$$\frac{\text{Orders delivered on-time}}{\text{Total orders received}} \times 100$$

2: Order completeness

The percentage of orders shipped complete with the first shipment. It is calculated by dividing total original order shipped complete by the total orders received.

$$\frac{\text{Orders delivered complete}}{\text{Total orders received}} \times 100$$

3: Error and damage free

Invoice adjustments/credit notes can be used as an indicator of the overall accuracy and quality of the order management and logistics process. It is calculated by dividing the number of 'clean' invoices by the total number of invoices raised.

$$\frac{\text{Clean invoices}}{\text{Total invoices}} \times 100$$

The computation of the index is achieved by multiplying the three scores together. Analysis can be done at the level of the individual customer, by channel, by region, by source of supply (e.g. distribution centre) or at any appropriate level.

Managing the processes that drive the perfect order

How can organizations get anywhere close to achieving the 'perfect order' on every occasion? The answer lies in some of the lessons to be learned from the excellent practitioners of 'total quality management' (TQM). For many years managers of production facilities have recognized that the only way that 100 per cent quality output can be achieved from any process is through the continuous control of that process. In other words, if the process is under control then the quality of the output can be guaranteed.

"if the process is under control then the quality of the output can be guaranteed"

Typically, in a production environment managers seeking to improve quality will seek to understand the critical elements of a process where, if a failure were to occur, the quality of the output would be affected. Then, having understood these critical potential 'fail points', the priority would be to monitor and control them constantly. More often that not, statistical process control (SPC) methods would be used to assist this task.

These same techniques of process control can be applied successfully to the control of service processes.

The first requirement is that the processes themselves are clearly understood and defined. Typically this will involve the detailed mapping and flow-charting of each aspect of the service processes – say, for example, the order management process. It is often the case that, once the results of these process mapping exercises are made visible, managers are surprised at the complexity of the processes. Indeed, a benefit of performing this exercise can be that resources are placed behind the re-engineering of those processes to simplify and streamline them.

The identification of the critical 'fail points' in a service process can be facilitated by the use of cause and effect analysis using a 'fishbone diagram'. This simple device is based upon the 80/20 concept that suggest that 80 per cent of the problems that arise in any process are the result of 20 per cent of the causes. In other words a few things seem to go wrong more often and cause most of the failures as a result.

If we take as an example an investigation into, say, failure to meet the customer's requested delivery date, we might find a number of more frequently occurring causes, e.g. product not available, carrier performance, lead-times too short and so on. If we then seek to investigate the reasons for each of these in turn, we can then identify the reasons for these failures. By

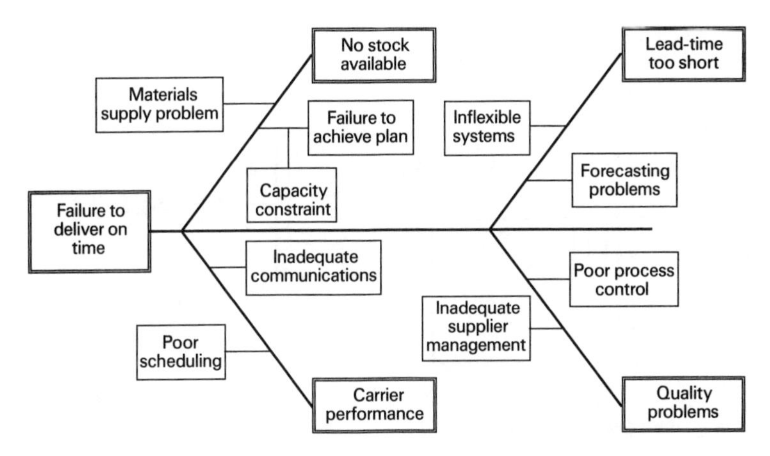

Figure 2.5 An example of cause and effect analysis using a fishbone diagram

plotting these causes and effects in the form of a fishbone diagram we can begin to identify the key areas where management attention must be focused if failure is to be reduced or eliminated. Figure 2.5 gives an example of a simplified fishbone diagram.

By focusing on the critical areas, ways will often be found to introduce 'fail-safe' systems. In any case if is vital that these critical points be monitored on a continuous basis so that potential problems can quickly be identified. The methods of statistical process control can be used to establish 'control limits' within which these activities must perform. Companies who are serious about perfect order achievement will also have a 'culture of measurement' and will incorporate these measures into their portfolio of key performance indicators.

An example of how one organization has established a set of key performance indicators from one end of the chain to the other is given in Figure 2.6. Here, the vital determinants of customer service performance are continually monitored and the measures are widely communicated and displayed at all levels in the business.

The underlying theme of this chapter has been that enduring customer relationships are based upon the continued delivery of superior service. To achieve the level and quality of service that customers require demands a clear understanding of the critical service issues market segment by market segment, combined with a commitment to the consistent achievement of the service promise.

"enduring customer relationships are based upon the continued delivery of superior service"

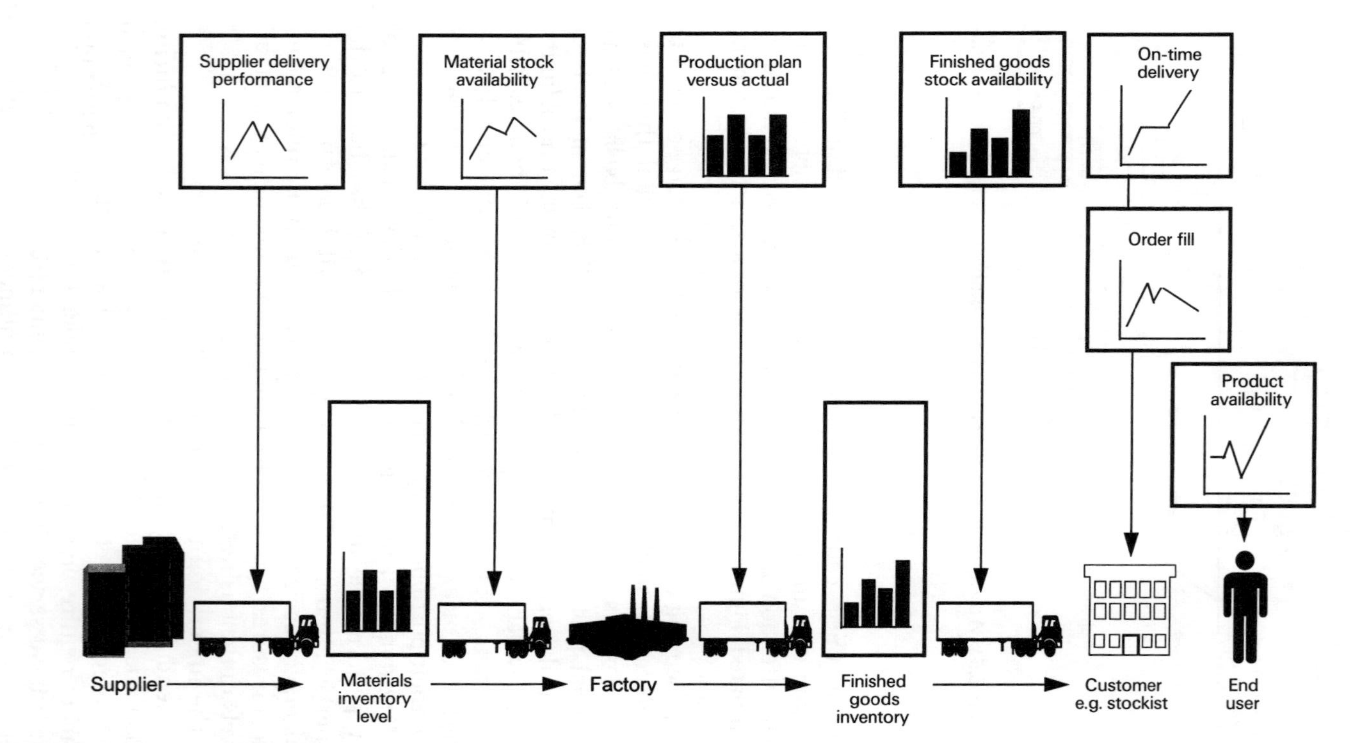

Figure 2.6 Process control and service quality

Chapter checklist Building customer relationships: key issues

- The importance of customer retention
  - Retained customers are more profitable
  - Calculate the lifetime value of a customer
  - Understand the reasons for customer defections

- The emerging concept of relationship marketing
  - The difference between a transaction and a relationship
  - Relationships as partnerships
  - Customer management becomes critical

- Developing a market-driven logistics strategy
  - Research customers' service needs
  - Define 'the perfect order'
  - Manage the processes that drive the perfect order

CHAPTER 3

Creating customer value

The most valuable asset in any business organization is the strength of its relationships with its customers. Long-term relationships are the basis for enhanced profitability. Such relationships however will only exist as long as the customer perceives there to be superior benefit arising from the arrangement. In today's market place the customer has become more demanding as expectations for product performance and service provision continue to increase. The power of the brand or corporate image has diminished as customers have developed in sophistication and in their recognition that there is almost always a choice.

To win and retain customers requires an understanding of what those customers *value* and a focus on the processes whereby that value can consistently be delivered. Clearly there is an equation between the value that customers perceive they are getting and the price they are prepared to pay. Hence the challenge is to identify ways in which customer value can be enhanced through marketing strategies that go beyond the traditional focus on brands and images.

The transition from brand value to customer value

There has been considerable discussion in recent years concerning a purported decline in the strength of brands. Evidence of the growing penetration of private labels and the willingness of customers to select from a portfolio of brands or suppliers adds to the view that the nature of brand loyalty has certainly changed. Whilst there can be no question that strong brands are still a significant asset to a business, whether it be consumer brands we are talking about or the 'corporate brand', it seems that in today's marketing environment there is a need to deliver more than just an image.

Many years ago Theodore Levitt introduced the idea of the 'augmented product' and this concept still holds good today. Essentially, the notion of the augmented product is that it is not sufficient to focus marketing effort around the tangible product features alone. Product features are quickly imitated or cloned by competitors and in any case, Levitt would argue, customers don't buy products they buy benefits. Instead the marketer needs to identify other ways in which value can be delivered to the customer over and above the intrinsic elements embedded in the product itself. Figure 3.1 depicts the idea of the augmented product as a 'halo' of benefits and services surrounding the core of functions and features.

This 'halo' obviously includes the intangible aspects of the brand image or 'personality'. However, the argument now is that whilst these brand values will always be important they are seldom enough. Instead they need to be augmented through the wider concept of *customer value*. The customer value concept recognizes that market-place success in the new competitive environment will require not only continued investment in the brand but also *investment in customers*. By 'customer' we mean the party or parties who actually buy the product as distinct from the consumer. The importance of this distinction is that much of marketing investment in the past has been aimed at consumers and not at the customer. Because of the shift in the balance of power in the distribution channels for most products it is important that we recognize that customers, not just consumers, have goals that they seek to achieve and that the role of the supplier is to help customers achieve those goals.

"customers, not just consumers, have goals that they seek to achieve"

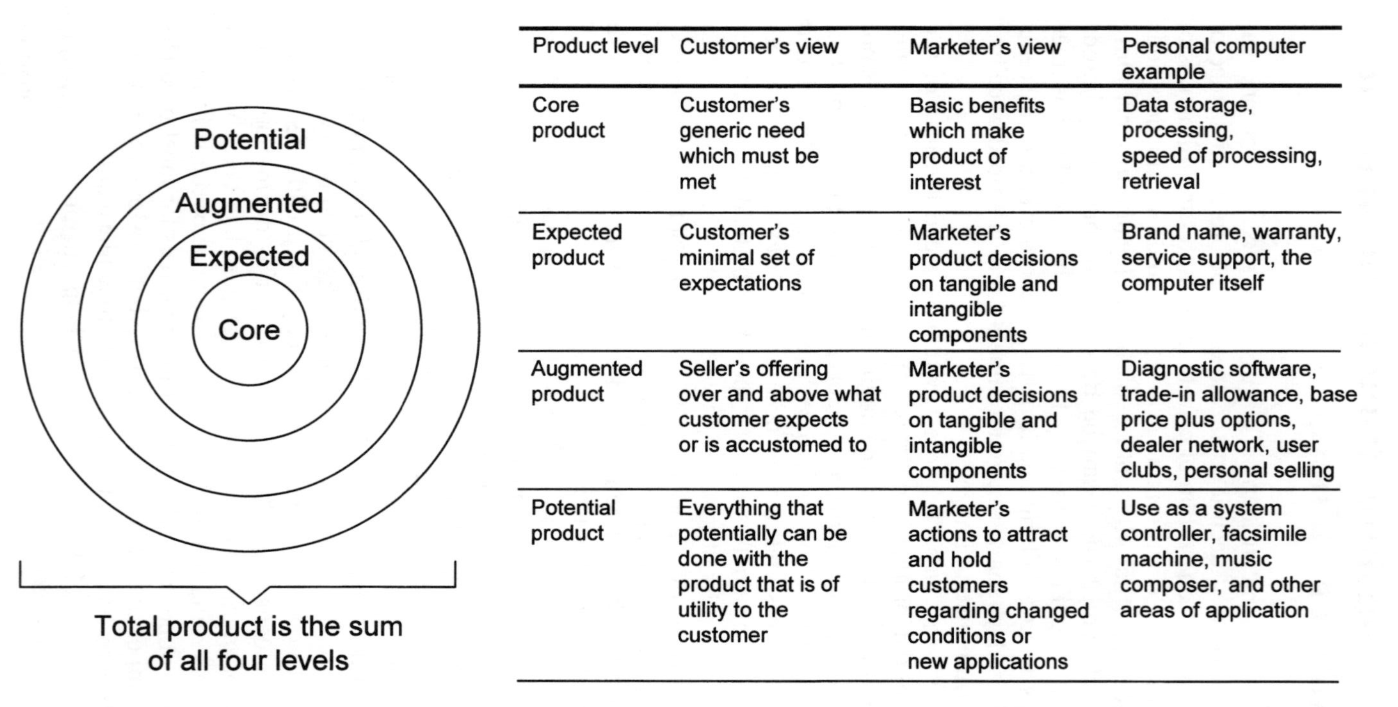

Product level	Customer's view	Marketer's view	Personal computer example
Core product	Customer's generic need which must be met	Basic benefits which make product of interest	Data storage, processing, speed of processing, retrieval
Expected product	Customer's minimal set of expectations	Marketer's product decisions on tangible and intangible components	Brand name, warranty, service support, the computer itself
Augmented product	Seller's offering over and above what customer expects or is accustomed to	Marketer's product decisions on tangible and intangible components	Diagnostic software, trade-in allowance, base price plus options, dealer network, user clubs, personal selling
Potential product	Everything that potentially can be done with the product that is of utility to the customer	Marketer's actions to attract and hold customers regarding changed conditions or new applications	Use as a system controller, facsimile machine, music composer, and other areas of application

Figure 3.1 The total product concept. *Source*: Collins, B. (1995) Chapter 11, Marketing for Engineers. In *Management for Engineers* (Sampson, D., ed.) Melbourne: Longman Cheshire, p. 415

Defining customer value

What actually is customer value? Put very simply, customer value is created when the perceptions of benefits received from a transaction exceed the total costs of ownership. The same idea can be expressed as a ratio:

$$\text{Customer value} = \frac{\text{Perceptions of benefits}}{\text{Total cost of ownership}}$$

'Total cost of ownership' rather than 'price' is used here because in most transactions there will be costs other than price involved. For example, inventory carrying costs, maintenance costs, running costs, disposal costs and so on. In business-to-business markets particularly, as buyers become increasingly sophisticated, the total cost of ownership can be a critical element in the purchase decision. 'Life-cycle costs', as they are referred to in the military and defence industries, have long been a critical issue in procurement decisions in those markets. Figure 3.2 shows the 'iceberg' effect of total costs of ownership where the immediate purchase price is the only aspect of cost that is visible, whereas below the surface of the water are all the costs that will follow as a result of the purchase decision.

The marketing task is to find ways to enhance customer value by improving the perceived benefits and/or reducing the total costs of ownership. Thus, the goal of marketing and logistics strategy should be to seek to maximize this ratio relative to that of competitors. It could be argued that logistics is

"The marketing task is to find ways to enhance customer value"

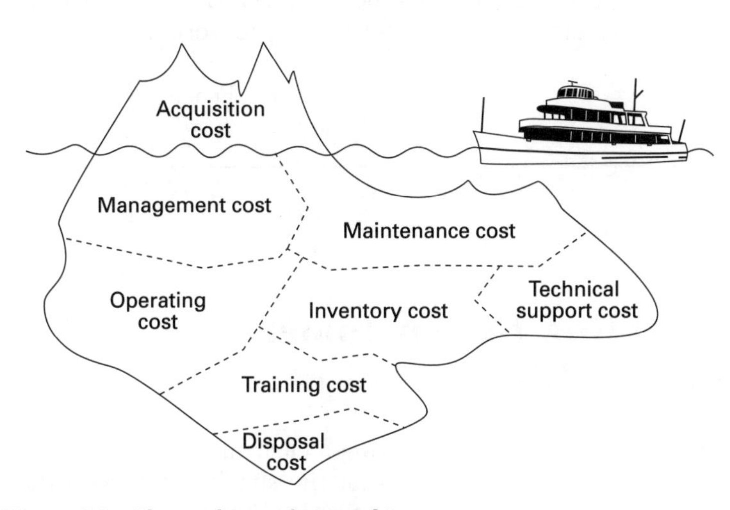

Figure 3.2 The total cost of ownership

almost unique in its ability to impact upon both the numerator and the denominator of this ratio. In the case of business-to-business marketing, higher customer value can be delivered through superior logistics performance enabling our customers to service their customers better but with less inventory and lower ordering costs for example. The same rationale of enhanced customer value applies to selling to end users where perhaps the benefits might come from, say, increased purchase convenience yet with lowered costs through improved payment terms.

The challenge within the supplying company is to identify unique ways to deliver this enhanced value that competitors will find difficult to imitate thus providing a basis for sustainable competitive advantage.

Procter and Gamble focus on customer value

'Good value is the foundation of our business. Our commitment to the essentials of good value have never been stronger. We are providing superior products at a competitive price by staying focused on the basics – continuous product innovation and relentless cost control.'

Procter & Gamble Annual Report 1995

'Redefining customer and consumer value means that we cannot charge for non-added value costs. This is the idea that is driving our strategy . . . and it's beginning to work like crazy.'

Ed Artz
CEO, Procter & Gamble
Quoted in *Fortune*, 7 March 1994

Impacting the customer's profitability

In business-to-business marketing a clear measure of customer value is given by the impact that the supplier has upon their customers' profitability. In other words if by our actions we can either increase the customers' chance of selling more product and/or reduce their costs of ownership then customer value has been created.

A good example of this is provided in marketing to the retail trade where increasingly 'return on shelf-space' is seen as a critical issue by the retailer.

Return on shelf-space can be expressed as:

$$\frac{\text{Profit}}{\text{Shelf-space}}$$

which can be further expressed as:

$$\frac{\text{Profit}}{\text{Sales}} \times \frac{\text{Sales}}{\text{Shelf-space}}$$

This is an important relationship since the first ratio (profit/sales) is more commonly referred to as 'the margin' and it is here that conventional buyer/supplier negotiations have focused.

However, by improving the second ratio (sales/shelf-space), which might be termed shelf-space productivity, then even a low margin can be leveraged into higher profitability. For example, many continental European discount retailers have net margins of 2 per cent or less, yet with high levels of sales per unit of shelf-space they can achieve a significant leverage as far as overall return on investment is concerned.

Thus to a supplier a strategy that focused upon improving the retailer's sales per square metre or per linear metre might win more of that shelf-space for their own products. There are a number of ways that such an improvement could be achieved. For example, by re-designing the pack so that it has a better 'footprint' on the shelf, occupying less space and at the same time developing a 'quick response' replenishment system so that the inventory velocity on the shelf is increased, the supplier can significantly impact shelf-space profitability.

More and more retailers are now starting to measure the profitability of their shelf-space, particularly as they move towards a strategy in which products are grouped into categories and those categories are then managed against profit goals. This idea of 'category management' will be explored further shortly.

"More and more retailers are now starting to measure the profitability of their shelf-space"

One tool that is widely used to assess shelf-space profitability is a measurement known as 'direct product profit' or 'DPP'. To a retailer direct product profit is a measure of an item's actual contribution to overall profit. It goes beyond the traditional measure of gross margin by:

- Adjusting the gross margin for each item to reflect deals, allowances, net forward buy income, prompt payment, discounts, etc.
- Identifying and measuring the costs that can be directly attributed to individual products (direct product costs like labour, space, inventory and transport).

The box entitled 'Direct product profit' describes the steps in moving from a crude gross margin measure to a more precise DPP.

Direct product profit

The net profit contribution from the sale of a product after allowances are added and all costs that can be rationally allocated or assigned to an individual product are subtracted.

	Sales
–	Cost of goods sold
=	Gross margin
+	Allowances and discounts
=	Adjusted gross margin
–	Warehouse costs
	• Labour (labour model – case, cube, weight)
	• Occupancy (space and cube)
	• Inventory (average inventory)
–	Transportation costs (cube)
–	Retail costs
	• Stocking labour
	• Front end labour
	• Occupancy
	• Inventory
=	Direct product profit

Because product characteristics and associated costs vary so much item by item (e.g. cube, weight, case pack count, handling costs, space occupied, turnover) the retailer needs to calculate the DPP at the item level. Similarly, because shelf-space is the limiting factor for the retailer the key measure of performance becomes DPP/square metre or even DPP/cubic metre.

The key issue to the retailer is 'shelf yield' which is calculated as follows:

$$\frac{\text{DPP per item} \times \text{Sales per week}}{\text{Square metres occupied}}$$

Thus, an item could have a low gross margin but have low direct product costs, high sales and low space occupancy so delivering a high shelf yield. Conversely a high gross margin product but with high direct product costs and low sales per week occupying more shelf space will deliver a low shelf yield.

Consequently the challenge to the supplier is to seek to develop products (including, crucially, the pack design) and logistics processes such that they deliver better shelf yield for the retailer. Companies like Procter & Gamble have consciously built issues like these into all their product and logistics strategies – even to the extent of re-designing the pack so that it improves the shelf-space occupancy.

By understanding in detail the customer's business, their cost structures and the dynamics of their markets, the supplier can begin to tailor their marketing logistics strategy so that significant improvements in customer value can be achieved. As the benefit to the customer starts to show through, so too should the return to the supplier in the shape of extra business.

Whilst return on shelf-space and DPP are issues specific to the retail sector, the general principle of focusing upon ways of positively impacting the customer's profit and loss account and their balance sheet is pivotal to the creation of customer value in any industry.

Figure 3.3 highlights some of the ways in which customer value can be enhanced by developing logistics processes that make it easier for the customer to service their customers whilst incurring less cost.

It may be necessary to 'educate' the customer who often will not have fully understood the real costs of their existing systems and processes. For example, many organizations still do not

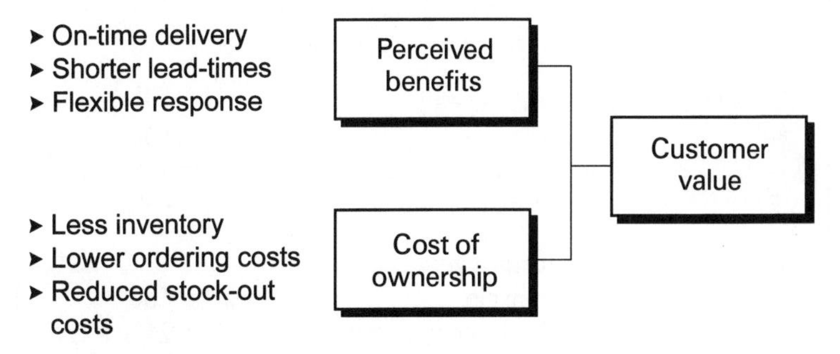

Figure 3.3 Logistics and customer value

"many organizations still do not recognize the true cost of carrying inventory"

recognize the true cost of carrying inventory. Whilst they may place a nominal working capital charge upon departments in relation to the inventory they hold, that charge rarely reflects the actual costs. It has been estimated that it costs an organization at least 25 per cent p.a. of the book value of its inventory to carry it in stock. Inventory here includes raw materials, components, work-in-progress, finished product as well as goods-in-transit. This figure of 25 per cent includes not only the cost of capital but the 'opportunity cost'. In other words the cost of the foregone return that could be made by investing that capital elsewhere. In addition there are the costs of storage and handling, obsolescence, stock losses, insurance and stock management.

Given that a medium to large organization will have inventory valued in millions of pounds, the annual carrying cost at 25 per cent will be considerable. The benefit of any reduction in that inventory will be two-fold: first a once-off release of cash and then second a continuing reduction in the annual cost of carrying that inventory which, other things being equal, should go direct to the bottom line.

The boxed example shows how a reduction in inventory can improve the profit margin.

How inventory carrying costs affect margins

Example: Direct cost of goods sold = £100
Selling price = £150
Inventory carrying cost = 24% p.a.

(i) With one stock turn a year
Gross margin = £50
Annual inventory carrying cost = £24
∴ gross margin less inventory cost = £26

(ii) With two stock turns a year
Gross margin = £50
Annual inventory carrying cost = 24/2 = £12
∴ gross margin less inventory cost = £38

(iii) With four stock turns a year
Gross margin = £50
Annual inventory carrying cost = 24/4 = £6
∴ gross margin less inventory cost = £44

(iv) With eight stock turns a year
Gross margin = £50
Annual inventory carrying cost = 24/8 = £3
∴ Gross margin less inventory cost = £47

Value-in-use

The whole issue of customer value is inevitably linked to price. Since price forms a part of the total cost of ownership it follows that there has to be a relationship between the price charged and the customer's perception of value. It also follows that the higher the perception of value the higher the price that can be charged. Conversely, if price exceeds the perceived value sales will probably decline. The case of Marlboro cigarettes has already been referred to in Chapter 1 but it provides a salutary lesson on what can happen when price and perceived value get out of line. Philip Morris, the manufacturer of Marlboro cigarettes, had for years traded on the success of that brand in the United States by progressively increasing the price ahead of inflation. At the same time greater competition was coming from lower priced brands and even retailers' own label products. During the 1980s the price of a pack of Marlboro cigarettes went up by 9.6 per cent a year, at the same time its market share slumped from 26.3 per cent in 1989 to 22.2 per cent in 1993. Concurrently, private label products grew to over 30 per cent of the market. Eventually in April 1993 the company was forced to cut the price by 20 per cent or 40 cents a pack – a move which triggered a major shock on Wall Street with the stocks of the top 25 consumer packaged goods companies collectively losing $50 billion in value, as investors feared for the future of branded products generally.

"the higher the perception of value the higher the price that can be charged"

The ultimate result of this significant re-adjustment of the price/value balance was that Marlboro regained the market share that it had lost, even though its profits were severely dented.

The moral of this story is that it is important to have a clear understanding of the value that customers (and consumers) place on an organization's offer. This can be termed 'value-in-use' and it should be a priority for all marketing managers to better understand the key elements that comprise it. Figure 3.4 highlights the idea of value-in-use as a balance between

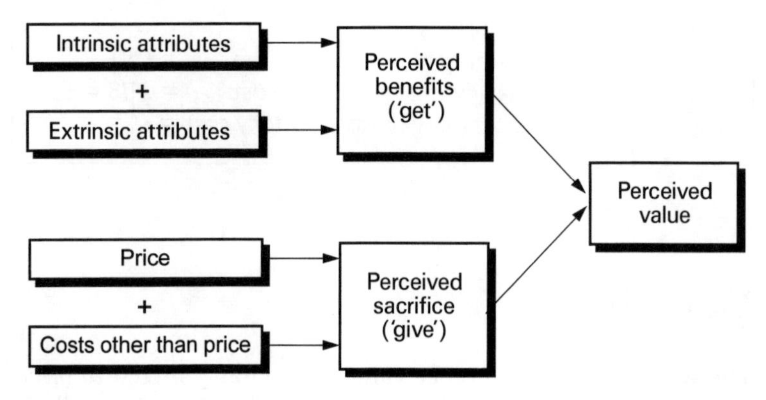

Figure 3.4 The components of value

perceived benefits (i.e. what the customer 'gets') and the perceived sacrifice (i.e. what the customer 'gives').

The perceived benefits derive from the hard, tangible elements of the offer – the intrinsic attributes – and the softer less tangible elements – the extrinsic attributes. The perceived sacrifice includes all those costs incurred by the customer, before, during and after the sale. Again, not all of these costs may be 'hard', some may be 'soft' such as perceived risk or the costs associated with the time consumed in the purchase process and so on.

It is important to recognize that in any given market there will probably be a number of segments who are quite different in their perceptions both of benefits and of sacrifice. In other words the weights that individual customers or consumers place upon the attributes of the offer will differ as will their perceptions of actual performance.

It is possible to measure the relative value that customers place upon the different attributes of an offer through the means of 'trade-off analysis'. Once we can identify the different 'value segments' that exist within a market then we can begin to develop marketing and logistics strategies specifically for those segments. Figure 3.5 offers a generic example of such a segmentation exercise in the car market.

This technique of mapping customer perceptions of benefit against their appraisal of total cost of ownership can provide a powerful basis for competitive analysis. Figure 3.6 suggests that if we measure both perceived benefits and total cost of ownership relative to competition then an acceptable position for an organization would be in the diagonal of the box. The lower right hand corner would reflect a perception of inferior value and likewise the top left corner a perception of superior value. Organizations finding themselves in this top left hand corner

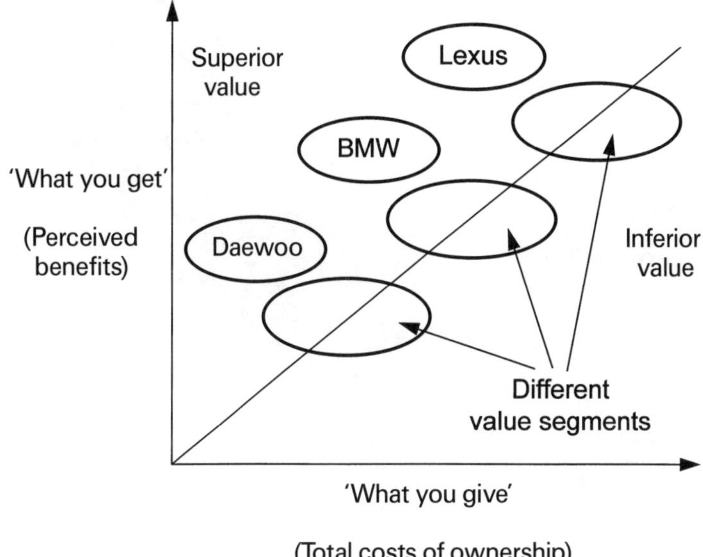

Figure 3.5 Value segmentation

might want to ensure that they are not 'giving the shop away'. In other words does their position of perceived superior value enable them to make an upwards price correction?

By focusing on those things the customer attaches most value to, the supplying organization is more likely to win and retain business. To do this requires an in-depth knowledge of the customers' own value chain. Thus, for example, if the customer is another business organization how do they create value for *their* customers? What are their customers' costs and what are the opportunities for those costs to be reduced through our intervention? What are the characteristics of their business processes and what possibilities exist for a greater integration of those processes with our own?

"By focusing on those things the customer attaches most value to, the supplying organization is more likely to win and retain business"

The same philosophy holds for marketing to end users. The supplying organization needs to understand the lifestyle of the consumer, the problems and pressures they face, the relative importance of time, the value they attach to convenience, ease of operation and so on. In this way a better targeting of customers can be achieved with value propositions that have specific relevance to the chosen segment. There may also be opportunities to emphasize total cost of ownership issues too. For example, a concentrated washing-up liquid that needs less liquid per wash, long-life light bulbs that need changing

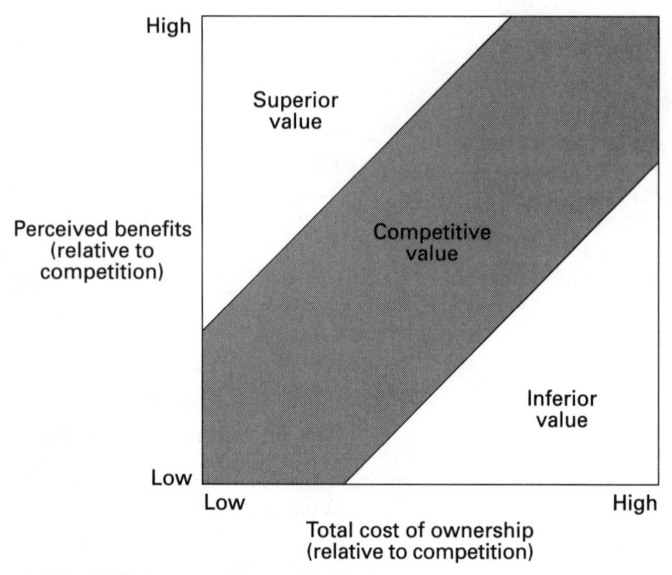

Figure 3.6 Relative customer value.

less often, paints that need no undercoats and oils that run cooler so few engine oil changes are needed.

Defining and delivering the value proposition

The value proposition is quite simply a statement of how, where and when value is to be created for specific customers or market segments. The value proposition should form the guiding principles around which all the activities of the firm are based, from product development to order fulfilment. It should also be reflected in the marketing communications strategy as well as underpinning the internal values of the business.

"The value proposition is a statement of how, where and when value is to be created for specific customers or market segments"

For a value proposition to provide a strong foundation for competitive advantage it must be defined from the customer's viewpoint. In other words: what will our offer do for customers that they will recognize as relevant to their needs? It must also be set against the backdrop of the explicit or implicit value propositions of competing offers. Once the value proposition is agreed, the challenge to logistics is to create and manage the processes that will deliver that value in a timely and consistent way. Linking logistics strategy and marketing strategy is of course the theme of this book and yet only rarely do we see the two managed on an integrated, customer value focused basis. One exception to this is provided by the UK-based car manufacturer, Rover Group Ltd. As the case study describes, the company established an over-riding marketing goal of supplying the customer with the car of their choice within 14 days. They then set about re-engineering their logistics and supply chain processes to make this value proposition a reality. When it is considered that there are literally millions of possible combinations of models, engine sizes, colours, options and so on, this is no mean feat.

Rover's market driven logistics

Up until 1993, the British-based car manufacturer Rover manufactured and marketed its product range in a way that was typical of its industry. It offered car buyers a range of models, each with a choice of body shells, engines, paint colours and finishes, levels of trim, and optional packages. In short, there were derivatives to suit every taste and every step of the company car buyers' corporate ladder. Prospective customers spent hours pawing over glossy brochures deciding exactly which of the thousands of possible variations they wanted to buy. Unfortunately, few ever got the car they had so carefully selected. They arrived in their local showroom to be met by a salesman avidly trying to sell the vehicles currently in stock. Often only those customers who were prepared to wait for several weeks, (most were not) eventually got the vehicle of their choice.

The underlying problem was that Rover, like most other car manufacturers, was operating an inefficient stock-push system, with customer dissatisfaction built-in. The whole system relied on elaborate, but inaccurate, best-guess forecasts of what Rover imagined its customers would want to buy, made 3–4 months ahead of the anticipated sales. A selection of these 'best-guess' vehicles were forwarded to dealers to be sold, the remainder waited in factory parking lots and disused airfields until the dealers could take them in. Attempts were made to build corrective measures into the last stage of the process, in the form of an electronic stock-swap support system that helped dealers to locate the more elusive variants. The system was successful in that it encouraged dealers to swap stock among themselves – to the point where one in every three vehicles sold in the UK was transferred between dealers on at least one occasion.

In addition to the cost of moving the stock around, there were interest charges to pay on up to half a billion pounds worth of unsold finished stock. Worse still, despite the expense and the dealers' best efforts, an independent industry-wide survey revealed that, ultimately only 25 per cent of customers ever got the car they really wanted. Rover concluded that the only way to remedy the situation was to devise a way to reverse the system based on a demand-pull logistics process.

Demand-pull starts with the customer, and market research showed that, while customer patience varies between markets, on average they were willing to wait for up to a fortnight for the right car. Rover's delivery times were a disappointing 6–8 weeks or longer, and had to be reduced. With this objective in mind Rover launched its 'Personal Production' programme. The name represented the programme's aspirations; first to provide every customer with the factory-fresh car of their choice, to be delivered anywhere in European within 14 days of order. Second, personal production aimed to involve directly all of the people in Rover's supply chain, from suppliers, through Rover itself, and on through the dealer network. With their cooperation Rover's production and logistics systems could be completely overhauled in pursuit of a strategy which combined standardization and simplification with flexibility.

Rover already knew that 80 per cent of sales come from 20 per cent of derivatives, and that these could be identified and built to forecast. It was therefore decided that these 'standard' vehicles should be held at central distribution points until confirmed customer orders called them through to the dealers. The dealers themselves initially resisted the notion of selling in a stockless environment, fearing that the cars might not materialize. However, the cars did arrive – 98 per cent of them within the set three-day target – and once the dealers had adjusted to the system, they began to appreciate its benefits.

The remaining 20 per cent of sales requiring less usual variants could – theoretically – be built to order at short notice. They would be given priority of production, and then dispatched from the factory directly to the dealers. It was the desire to deliver this 20 per cent within the target 14 days that really drove through significant changes in Rover's production practices.

Wherever possible, components and whole new cars were designed to allow maximum compatibility across the model ranges, with the shortest possible lead-times. Meeting these criteria demanded a change in Rover's manufacturing costing mind-set, from the pursuit of the lowest component unit costs to lowest overall manufacturing cost. For example, the Rover 200's choice of 85 different wiring harnesses was reduced to a handful of individually more expensive but more flexible options. Increasingly, Rover looked to its suppliers to deliver solutions to its component needs, working with them to reduce overall parts counts, shorten process times, and develop late configuration capability.

As personal production progressed, the percentage of Rover cars made to order gradually increased, reaching 30 per cent after two years. Stock turn increased from 4 to 5 times per year, and stocks of finished vehicles were reduced by 20 per cent. Meanwhile Rover has advanced steadily towards its 14 day delivery target.

Source: Based on material contained in a speech by John Towers, Rover CEO, Brussels, 1996.

The means by which value is 'delivered' to customers is clearly critical to maintaining competitive advantage. When we talk of delivery systems we refer not only to the physical delivery of products or the presentation of service, but also to the marketing channels employed, the flexibility of response, the linking of buyer/supplier logistics and information systems and so on. In other words the design of the value delivery system should be seen as a powerful means of engineering stronger linkages between the customer's and the supplier's value chains. One company that has taken the customer, and consumer, value issue seriously is Procter & Gamble (P&G) who have re-directed their entire business focus towards competing through enhanced customer value. One way in which this has manifested itself in North America is through their strategy of 'every-day low price' (EDLP) or 'value pricing'. In an attempt to reduce the prices of their products to consumers, thus enhancing the value, P&G sought to remove significant cost from the supply chain – their estimate was that logistics costs in the US came to $1 billion a year on sales of $15 billion.

Much of this cost was generated as the result of promotional activity, both from promotions aimed at the trade as well as at end users. For example wherever promotional price cuts in wholesale prices were made – which was frequently – retailers would take advantage of these mark-downs by 'forward buying'.

In other words they would buy more than they required for immediate sales requirements and then sell the remaining goods at full price later. This would lead to big surges in demand in one period to be followed by a downturn in demand in the next. As a result some P&G factories were only running at 35 to 65 per cent of their rated efficiency. On top of this, the company estimated that it was making 55 daily price changes on some 80 brands leading to order inaccuracy and invoice errors. The real costs of these promotions were significant and far outweighed any tactical sales advantage.

The idea behind EDLP or value pricing is to offer a guaranteed low price to the trade for a fixed contractual period. This price will be lower than the previous list price but will not fluctuate during the contract period. Neither will there be tactical price promotions. As a result both parties should benefit – as well as the final consumer.

In Chapter 4 we will explore in more detail the ways in which significant additional costs can be generated throughout a supply chain as the result of swings in demand – the sort of swings brought about by promotional activity. It will be apparent that anything that can be done to reduce those fluctuations – which increase in magnitude as they flow backwards through the supply chain – will have a beneficial effect on capacity utilization, inventory and hence costs.

Customer management

The implications for the supplier of the adoption of the customer value concept as the driving force for marketing strategy are considerable. In particular it suggests that a more proactive approach to the management of customer relationships must be assumed. The idea behind *customer management* is that the supplier actively seeks to better understand the customer's business and the needs of their customers and then develops total business solutions in partnership with the customer. Perhaps the best examples come from manufacturers supplying retailers, although the same principles could be applied in any business-to-business context.

"a more proactive approach to the management of customer relationships must be assumed"

In retailing, as we have previously observed, there is an growing trend towards *category management* which essentially focuses around enhancing the profitability of a related family of products. A large retail store might well have over 200 categories ranging from 'oral care' to 'oven-ready meals'. In the oral care category, for example, decisions will have to be taken on the breadth and the depth of the merchandise stocked. Not just the question of how many brands of toothpaste should be carried, but also range decisions on toothbrushes, toothpicks, mouth washes, dental floss and so on. Furthermore, how much space should be given to each item and brand within the category and what position should they occupy upon the shelf? Decisions taken on these issues can have a significant effect on profitability across the category as a whole.

In this example a proactive customer management strategy developed by a supplier within that category might involve conducting in-store research to observe how shoppers react to different lay-outs, post-purchase interviews to determine how choices are actually made and the analysis of electronic point of sales (EPOS) data to analyse cross-purchasing patterns (i.e. what products tend to be purchased along with other products).

The proactive supplier would seek to become the expert on the categories in which it competes enabling the retailer to enhance their profitability as a result. The argument is that the supplier is usually best placed to be the category expert as they tend only to compete in a limited number of categories whilst the retailer will of necessity be concerned with several hundred categories.

In other types of environment the concept of customer management is also relevant. For example, in the case of an electronic component manufacturer supplying a distributor, the supplier might seek to use the distributor's sales data to better manage the flow of product into distribution centres. In Chapter 4 we will examine how this idea can be developed through the principle of 'vendor managed inventory'.

A further dimension of customer management is that it seeks to focus the resources of the business upon those customers where either current or potential profitability is highest. Underlying this idea is the well known 80/20 principle or the Pareto rule. The 80/20 principle tells us that not only is 80 per cent of the total sales volume of a business generated by just 20 per cent of the customers but that the likelihood is that 80 per cent of the total costs of servicing all the customers will be caused by only 20 per cent of the customers (but probably not the same 20 per cent). Whilst the proportion may not be exactly 80/20 it will generally be in that region.

Figure 3.7 illustrates the shape of the distribution of profits that result from the uneven spread of revenues and costs across the customer base. From this example, it will be seen that there

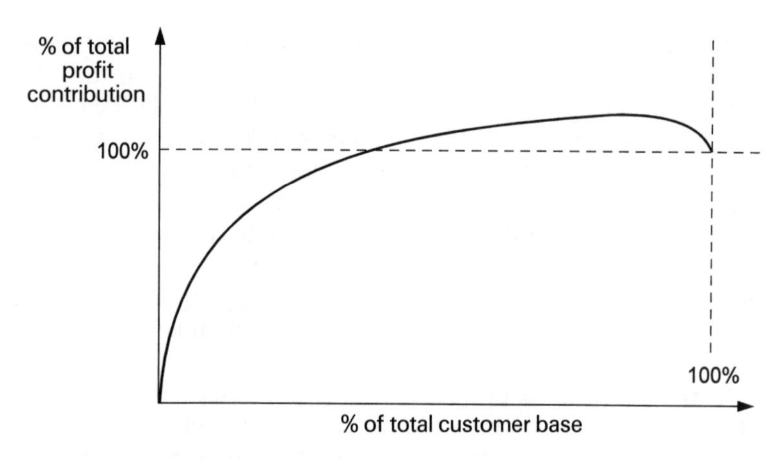

Figure 3.7 Customer profitability

is a 'tail' of customers who are actually unprofitable and who therefore reduce total profit contribution!

The challenge to customer management therefore is first to identify the real profitability of customers and second to develop logistics strategies that will improve the profitability of all customers.

"Why should customers differ in their real profitability?"

Why should customers differ in their real profitability?

The first reason is that different customers will often buy a different mix of products and because individual products have different gross margins then clearly the mix of products purchased will impact upon the profitability of specific customers.

Beyond this however it must be recognized that there are also substantial differences in the costs of servicing individual customers. It has been said that 'Profitability is largely determined by what happens *after* the point of production'.

The costs of service begin with the order itself – what time does the sales person spend with the customer; is there a key account manager whose time is spent wholly or in part working with that customer; what commissions do we pay on these sales?

Then there are the order processing costs which themselves will differ according to the number of lines on the order, the number of orders and their complexity. Beyond this there will be transport costs, materials handling costs and often inventory and warehousing costs – particularly if the products are held on a dedicated basis for customers, e.g. as with own-label products.

With many customers it will often be the case that the supplying company is allocating specific funds for customer promotions, advertising support, additional discounts and the like. In the case of promotions (e.g. a special pack for a particular retailer) there will most likely be additional hidden costs to the supplier. For example, the disruption to production schedules and the additional inventory holding cost is rarely accounted for and assigned to customers.

The basic principle of customer profitability analysis is that the supplier should seek to assign all costs that are specific to individual accounts. A useful test to apply when looking at these costs is to ask the question: 'What costs would I avoid if I didn't do business with this customer?'

The benefit of using the principle of 'avoidability' is that many costs of servicing customers are actually shared amongst several or many customers. The warehouse is a good example – unless the supplier could release warehousing space for other purposes then it would be incorrect to allocate a proportion of the total warehousing costs to a particular customer.

A checklist of costs to include when drawing up the 'profit and loss account' for specific customers is given in the box.

The customer profit and loss account

Revenues
- Net sales value

Less
Costs
(attributable costs only)
- Cost of sales (actual product mix)
- Commissions
- Sales calls
- Key account management time
- Trade bonuses and special discount
- Order processing costs
- Promotional costs (visible and hidden)
- Merchandising costs
- Non-standard packaging/unitization
- Dedicated inventory holding costs
- Dedicated warehouse space
- Materials handling costs
- Transport costs
- Documentation/communications costs
- Returns/refusals
- Trade credit (actual payment period)

Whilst it may not be practicable to undertake such analysis for individual accounts, it should be possible to select representative customers on a sample basis so that a view can be gained of the relative costs associated with different types of accounts or distribution channels or even market segments.

The recommended procedure for implementing customer profitability analysis is highlighted in the flowchart shown as Figure 3.8. What will often emerge from these studies is that the largest customers in terms of volume, or even revenue, may not be the most profitable because of their high costs of service. Thus it may be that the larger customers gain larger volume-based discounts, they require more frequent deliveries to more dispersed locations and they may insist on non-standard pallets, for example.

What ultimately should be the purpose of this analysis? Ideally we require all our customers to be profitable in the medium to long term and where customers currently are profitable we should seek to build and extend that profitability further.

The customer profitability matrix illustrated in Figure 3.9 provides some generalized guidance for strategic direction. Briefly the appropriate strategies for each quadrant of the matrix are:

Build These customers are relatively cheap to service but their net sales value is low. Can volume be increased without a proportionate increase in the costs of service? Can our sales team be directed to seek to influence these customers' purchases towards a more profitable sales mix?

Danger zone These customers should be looked at very carefully. Is there any medium to long term prospect either of improving net sales value or reducing the costs of service? Is there a strategic reason for keeping them? Do we need them for their volume even if their profit contribution is low?

Cost engineer These customers could be more profitable if the costs of servicing them could be reduced. Is there any scope for increasing drop sizes? Can deliveries be consolidated? If new accounts in the same geographic area were developed would it make delivery more economic? Is there a cheaper way of gathering orders from these customers, e.g. telesales?

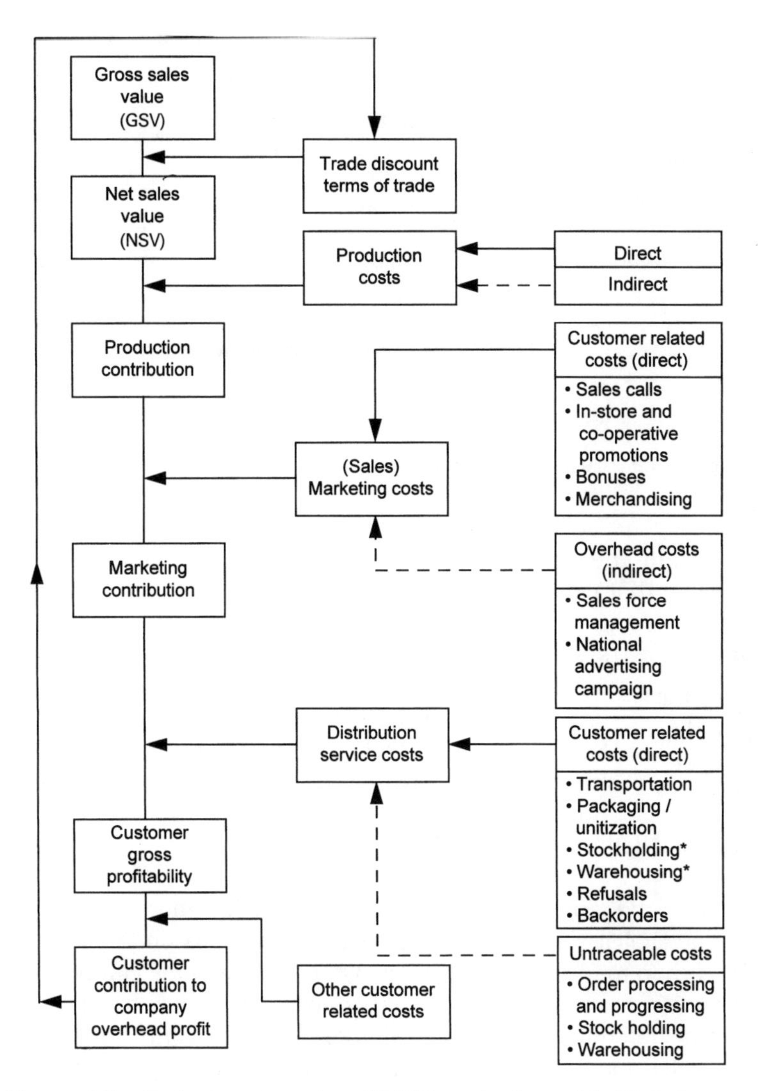

Figure 3.8 Customer account profitability: a basic model. *Only in certain circumstances

Protect The high net sales value customers who are relatively cheap to service are worth their weight in gold. The strategy for these customers should be to seek relationships which make the customer less likely to want to seek alternative suppliers. At the same time we should constantly seek opportunities to develop the volume of business that we do with these customers whilst keeping strict control of costs.

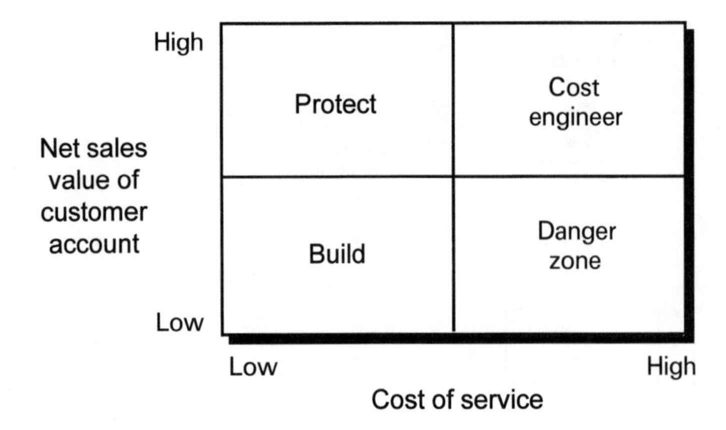

Figure 3.9 Customer profitability matrix

Ideally the organization should seek to develop an accounting system that would routinely collect and analyse the data on customer profitability. Unfortunately most accounting systems are product focused rather than customer focused. Likewise cost reporting is traditionally on a functional basis rather than a transactional basis. So, for example, we know the costs of the transport function as a whole or of making a particular product. What we do not know though, are the costs of delivering a specific mix of product to a particular customer.

"most accounting systems are product focused rather than customer focused"

The challenge to any business is to define more clearly the value that it seeks to provide for its chosen customer segments and then to focus on the means whereby that value can be delivered most cost effectively. Customer value has become the major differentiator in many markets and the contribution that logistics can make to enhancing that differentiation is now more widely recognized within the leading companies.

Chapter checklist Creating customer value: key issues

- The change in emphasis from brand value to customer value
  - Customer value is the difference between perceived benefits and total cost
  - Focus on the value proposition
  - Understand the customer's value chain

- Can we impact the customer's costs of ownership?
  - Reduce their costs of stockholding
  - Reduce their stock out costs
  - Improve their 'direct product profit'

- Customer management
  - The trend towards category management
  - Understanding the costs-to-serve
  - Differentiate service strategy according to customer priority

CHAPTER 4

The move to supply chain management

The emergence of the 'network organization' is a recent phenomenon that has given rise to much comment and analysis. These 'virtual' organizations are characterized by a confederation of specialist skills or capabilities provided by the network members. It is argued that such collaborative arrangements provide a more effective means of satisfying customer needs at a profit than does the single firm undertaking multiple value-creating activities. The implications of the network organization for marketing management are considerable and, in particular, the challenges to logistics management are profound.

To make networks more effective in satisfying end-user requirements requires a high level of cooperation between organizations in the network and the recognition of the need to make inter-firm relationships mutually beneficial. Underpinning the successful network organization is the value-added exchange of information between partners. Creating 'visibility' along the pipeline ensures that the manufacture and delivery of product can be driven by real demand rather than by a forecast and hence enables all parties in the chain to operate more effectively.

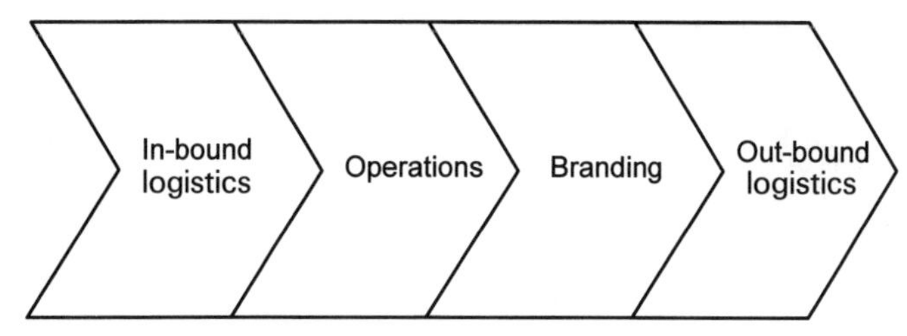

Figure 4.1 The value chain

Many changes in our understanding of industrial organizations have occurred in the last few decades but perhaps one of the most profound has been the recognition that even the largest business will only have relatively few competencies in which it can claim real distinction. This realization has led to an increasing concern by management to focus on the 'core business' and to 'outsource' everything else. Inevitably, as this process of retrenchment and outsourcing gathers pace, the management of relationships between partners in the network becomes paramount.

Michael Porter, one of the leading thinkers in the development of our understanding of the foundation of competitive advantage, was one of the first to draw our attention to the importance of the *value chain.*

The value chain represents all the activities that take place within the firm to create value for customers. In the classic view of the organization we could describe purchasing, production, marketing and distribution as the basic steps in the value creation process which is portrayed in Figure 4.1.

"The value chain represents all the activities that take place within the firm to create value for customers"

The fundamental importance of this concept is that it forces us to look at every step in the chain and to ask the question 'are we creating customer value as cost-effectively as possible?'. Thus each activity should be analysed in terms of what it is doing for the customer and what costs it is incurring for the business. An argument that increasingly is being heard is that if the organization identifies an activity where it does not have a competitive advantage in terms of cost-effectiveness, then it should contemplate finding a partner who could perform that activity more cheaply and/or more effectively. Thus many companies have chosen to outsource their transportation and warehousing activities for example.

This analysis however, needs to be extended to include an understanding of the *strategic importance* of these value creating activities. By definition, all stages of the value chain are potentially strategically important in the sense that if a

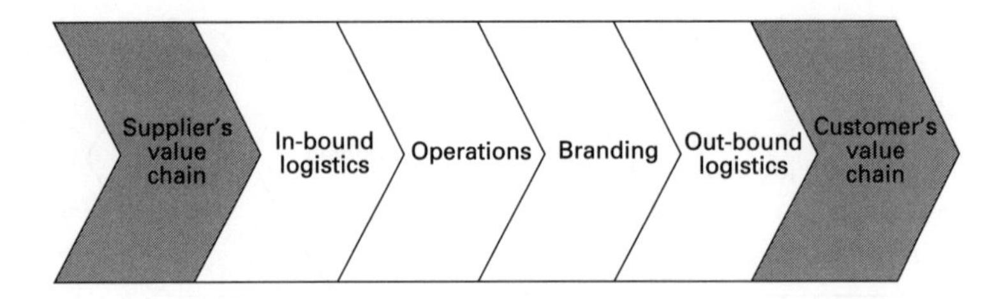

Figure 4.2 The extended value chain

"all stages of the value chain are potentially strategically important"

competitor consistently outperforms us in any one of the value-creating activities in the chain then we are vulnerable. This need not deter the organization from seeking to find partners to perform value creating activities on its behalf – indeed it can be argued that it strengthens the case for out-sourcing. What it does imply however is that the organizations to which these critical tasks are out-sourced must not be seen as sub-contractors but rather as true partners in an *extended value chain* (Figure 4.2).

The parallels between the management of relationships in an industrial network and the concept of supply chain management are apparent. Supply chain management is concerned to achieve a more cost-effective satisfaction of end customer requirements through buyer–supplier process integration. This integration is typically achieved through a greater transparency of customer requirement through the sharing of information. This integration is subsequently compounded through the establishment of 'seamless' processes that link the identification of a physical replenishment need with a 'just-in-time' response.

The important concept here is the idea of *process integration.* Processes are the fundamental ways through which value is created. Process management is addressed in more detail in Chapter 7; however, the key issue is that processes are 'horizontal' in that they cut across traditional 'vertical' functions. Typically processes include: new product development, order fulfilment, supplier management and customer management. To achieve real integration in the supply chain requires ideally that these processes also be integrated – upstream with suppliers and downstream with customers. Take, for example, the new product development process. If suppliers as well as customers can become part of an integrated process team (as now happens increasingly in the car industry) then it is more likely that innovative products meeting the needs of customers and consumers will be developed – and at greater profit to the members of the integrated chain.

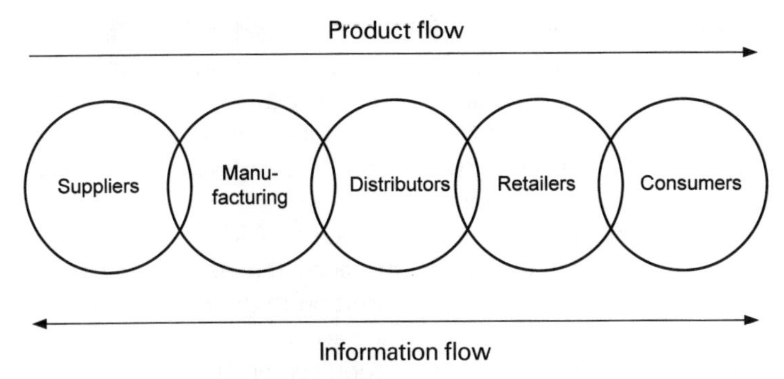

Figure 4.3 Supply chain integration

The same argument is true for all processes, i.e. that integration upstream and downstream will lead to a more responsive supply chain, an integration that is underpinned by the recognition of the need for mutual benefit which is made possible by the free flow of information up and down the chain.

Simultaneous with the growth in supply chain integration has been a move towards rationalization of the supplier base. In other words organizations have actively sought to reduce the number of suppliers they do business with. The motivations for this move towards supplier rationalization are based partly upon economics, partly upon the search for continuous quality improvement and innovation but also on a realization that there is a limit to the extent to which multiple supplier relationships can be effectively managed.

"organizations have actively sought to reduce the number of suppliers they do business with"

Car part makers 'face challenge'

Motor components suppliers are presented with an unprecedented challenge to invest in information technology or face extinction, according to a report to be published next week.

The study from Euromonitor Reports warns that even if the estimated 30,000 medium-sized automotive component makers in this country react quickly, three-quarters will go out of business within 10 years.

A trend towards fewer suppliers means most of the £200 billion turnover sector is engaged in a competition for survival, of which creating electronic links with the customer is the first round. European suppliers are in a similar battle, says the report, although ignorance of the requirement is more pronounced here.

Component suppliers that adopt electronic data interchange – allowing messages to be passed rapidly to and from their customers – will also need to invest in new manufacturing methods, including cell manufacturing, multi-skilled workforces and just-in-time supply and delivery systems, to make use of the improved information flows.

Almost all first-tier suppliers, such as GKN, Robert Bosch and Lucas Industries, have embraced the new systems and reduced costs which can be passed on to the car-maker. They can also respond rapidly and accurately to car-makers' requirements and enjoy longer contract terms.

Rover is highlighted as having worked with suppliers to cut the time between receiving a dealer order to delivery time to 10 days.

Daily Telegraph, 23 March 1995 © Telegraph Group Ltd, London 1996

As a result of these changes in the supply chain there has emerged a growing inter-dependency amongst the parties in the chain. With this inter-dependency has come a realization that cooperation and partnership are essential pre-requisites for the achievement of long-term mutual benefit.

"If supply chains are to operate as seamless processes then they require openness, trust and a willingness to share information"

This move towards the creation of what has been called 'the boundary-less business' or the 'virtual corporation' requires a fundamental transformation in the way in which upstream and downstream relationships are viewed. There is no room for the traditional, adversarial buyer/supplier relationship. If supply chains are to operate as seamless processes then they require openness, trust and a willingness to share information.

The boundary-less business

In a boundary-less company, suppliers aren't 'outsiders'. They are drawn closer and become trusted partners in the total business process. Customers are seen for what they are – the livelihood of a company. Customers' vision of their needs and the company's view become identified, and every effort of every man and woman in the company is focused on satisfying those needs.

> In a boundary-less company, internal functions begin to blur. Engineering doesn't design a product and then 'hand-it-off' to manufacturing. They form a team along with marketing and sales, finance and the rest. Customer service? It's not somebody's job. It's everybody's job.
>
> *John F. Welch*, Chairman and CEO, GE Annual Report 1990
> Quoted in Frederick E. Webster, *Market-Driven Management*,
> John Wiley, 1994

This progression towards supply chain thinking is evidenced by various initiatives at company, industry and even governmental level to establish the philosophy and practice of *partnership sourcing* which is characterized by a focus on such things as:

- Early involvement of suppliers in the new product development process.
- Joint programme of continuous product and process improvement facilitated by transparency of cost in both directions.
- Agreement of performance targets and measurement criteria.
- Commitment to the open flow of information facilitated by the use of electronic data interchange (EDI).

The two keys to successful partnership relationships, based on trust and commitment to shared goals, are transparency of cost and shared information on demand and supply issues.

(i) Cost transparency

Cost transparency or 'open-book accounting' refers to the process through which suppliers share information on the cost structures of their product with their customers. The purpose behind this is to identify the opportunities where joint action could reduce or eliminate some of those supplier costs. The aim of the buyer – as it always has been – is to reduce the cost of purchased items.

However, under this new philosophy price reductions come not at the expense of the supplier's margin – as they traditionally have done – but instead they are achieved through reductions in the supplier's costs.

For example, significant cost savings might be realized if the supplier were able to achieve better utilization of capacity through advance notification of customer requirements. The costs to the supplier of 'schedule instability' are hidden in the loss of economies of scale, in quality costs, and in the higher costs of overtime for labour.

"The use of activity based costing (ABC) may enable both suppliers and customers better to understand the real sources of costs in the supply chain"

Often the costing systems used by suppliers may not reflect the true costs and hence may mislead managers in their search for cost reduction. For example, if the supplier is using conventional allocation methods to deal with fixed costs – perhaps based upon direct labour hours – this could lead to an under- or over-statement of the true costs. The use of activity based costing (ABC) may overcome this and enable both suppliers and customers better to understand the real sources of costs in the supply chain.

Opportunities for significant process improvements can also be identified through the clearer understanding of where value-adding time and non-value adding time is being consumed. These opportunities will be more visible the greater the willingness to share cost information between parties in the supply chain. It should also be emphasized that the transparency should be in both directions. Thus as well as the customer being able to see clearly the supplier's costs structures, the supplier needs to understand how the customer's own processes are managed, the role that is played by the product being supplied and the requirements of the customer's own customers for service and product functionality.

Open-book accounting

Open-book accounting is the name given to the negotiation technique in which the customer requires the supplier to share component cost information, as part of the process of improvement and cost reduction.

The problems which have dogged this practice stem from a lack of respect and trust. Customers tend to require the supplier to share all information – rather than just that which is relevant to the process – often providing little justification except the general claim that it is a necessary part of supply chain management.

There are many different approaches taken by vehicle manufacturers to open-book negotiation and it appears that major problems are caused by the diversity of cost accounting systems. At present it is evident that within large divisional firms (customers and suppliers) there may be many different systems, not necessarily compatible with one another. The problem is clearly compounded when two separate firms try to compare notes: arguments arise over who is actually reducing costs, etc.

Open-book negotiation is linked with the concept of supplier development – in which customers try to help their suppliers to make improvements in their processes and management.

There are two distinct types of approach observable in customers. The most common is based upon crudely expressed pressure for price reduction – leading to increases in productivity. Less evident is the development of genuine 'partnership' policies, which lead to joint efforts on removing costs from product design and processes. Such practices appear to be in transition phase although both (or either) could be part of long-term relationships. It appears likely that the supplier's ability to provide the lowest price for a component of a system will become a 'given' – in the same way that sustainable product quality has developed into a qualifying criterion.

Source: A Review of the Relationships between Vehicle Manufacturers and Suppliers, Department of Trade and Industry, February 1994

(ii) Shared information

What distinguishes true supply chain integration from looser and more transient arrangements is the willingness of the parties in the chain to share information, in particular information relating to demand, on-hand inventories and supply or manufacturing schedules. The aim is to create an 'information highway' which links the final market place with all the upstream players enabling all parties to manage their logistics to better effect, i.e. lower costs yet higher levels of responsiveness.

Later in this chapter we will explore some of the breakthroughs that are being achieved through the creation of such information highways along the supply chain. The fundamental concept is that organizations in the chain seek to create additional customer value through the exchange of information. Such a process can be referred to as the *value-added exchange of information.*

For example, by sharing information on current usage or offtake with its suppliers, a customer can enable those suppliers to anticipate future requirements – hence better cost efficiencies at the supplier level should be achievable. The earlier that this information can be shared and the more widespread is its dissemination up the chain, the greater will be these opportunities for efficiency improvements.

It will be apparent that such an exchange of information will only be possible if there is a high degree of trust and commitment between the various parties in the chain. The problem is that, traditionally, relationships between buyers and suppliers have tended to be adversarial rather than co-operative and to be based more upon a 'win-lose' mentality rather than the ideal 'win-win' mind set.

"traditionally, relationships between buyers and suppliers have tended to be adversarial"

There are however, signs that as organizations come to recognize that competing in today's more challenging market place requires ever-higher levels of responsiveness achieved at lower cost, they will also be forced to create more responsive pipelines. The key to the achievement of these more flexible, faster and low-cost pipelines is information exchange. Without that exchange it is unlikely that these new competitive challenges can be met.

The implications of this growth of collaborative supply chain networks for competitive strategy are considerable – in particular the likelihood that real competitive advantage will, in the future, derive from the supply chain as a whole rather than the individual components of it. In other words 'supply chains compete, not companies'. The need to structure supply chain management into overall business strategy development becomes ever more apparent. Furthermore there will be advantage to be gained through the proactive leadership of the supply chain network – in effect by the assumption of the role of supply chain 'captain'.

Creating 'lean' supply chains

One of the fundamental drivers of supply chain integration is the realization that 'lean logistics' is a vital pre-requisite for market responsiveness. Traditional inventory-based systems that sought to anticipate customer requirements through sales forecasts have been challenged by the advent of just-in-time, quick response solutions which rely on information rather than inventory to meet customers' needs. 'Substituting information for inventory' has become the guiding principle for logistics managers in those organizations that seek

" 'Substituting information for inventory' has become the guiding principle for logistics managers"

to achieve flexible and timely response in volatile and short life-cycle markets. The concept of the 'time-based competitor' is now firmly established and time compression through the early capture of real customer demand is a key element of this concept.

Because conventional supply chains comprise separate corporate entities with only minimal up-stream and down-stream transparency of market-related information, they inevitably have to buffer themselves against uncertainly of demand by holding inventory. As a result these supply chains carry inventory far in excess of current requirements with duplication of stock at each buyer/supplier interface. Not only is this a significant burden in terms of working capital but, even more importantly, such chains are slow to respond to volatile demand. An analogy can be drawn with an oil pipeline that is lengthy and slow moving and in which the oil must pass through many intermediate storage tanks before finally reaching the end market. If the customers' requirements for the type and grade of oil were to change frequently, the supplying company would face significant problems in meeting those requirements.

A further problem with supply chains with numerous buffers between the two ends of the chain is that small changes in demand in the final market place are amplified and distorted as they move back through the chain. This is the well-known 'Forrester Effect' named after the MIT professor who first identified it and it is the cause of considerable hidden cost to the supply chain as a whole.

The Forrester effect has its roots in the fact that in a chain of several players, each acting independently of each other and probably only sharing minimal, if any, information, the likelihood is that even small changes in end user demand will result in amplified demand the further upstream the surge travels. The causes of this 'tidal wave' or 'bull-whip' phenomenon are based primarily on the fact that independent inventories at each step in the chain act as buffers that distort and amplify requirements and, in effect, 'hide' real demand from upstream suppliers.

Let us take a simple example. Market research suggests that the cat owners in the United Kingdom who buy tinned cat food feed their cats about the same amount every day. However, most of these cat owners do not buy in single cans but in multiples with a delay between subsequent purchase occasions. Similarly the retail store at which they buy these products order by the pallet load or even the truck load, and again at varying frequencies. Other distribution channels such as wholesalers and cash and carry will also be ordering according to

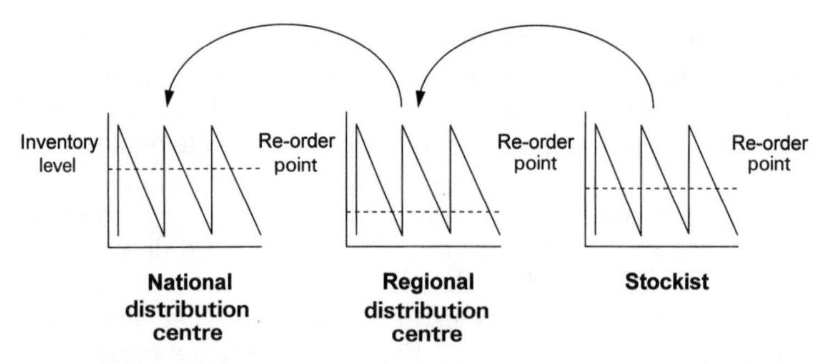

Figure 4.4(a) Inventory hides demand

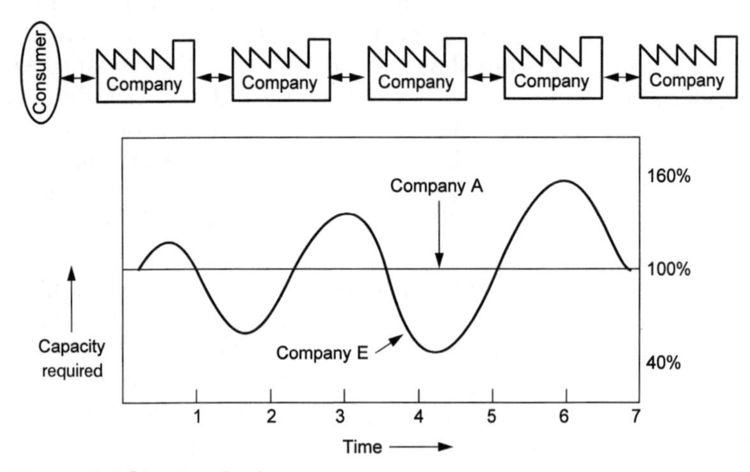

Figure 4.4(b) Supply chain interactions cause upstream fluctuations

their own re-order level policies and, of course, significant promotional activity will be taking place almost continuously, creating a lot of temporary brand switching amongst cat owners and/or forward buying by retailers and wholesalers.

The combined effect of all of this is to create a very volatile picture of demand by the time this filtered and distorted picture is received at the cat food factory! Of course, things become even more distorted as these demands are translated into upstream requirements for raw materials, packaging products and so on.

Figure 4.4(a) demonstrates how at each stage in the chain, inventory first hides demand and then leads to a 'lumpy' and lagged order on the next upstream party in the chain. Figure 4.4(b) illustrates how small changes in demand in the end-user market can create significant oscillations the further up the chain we go.

To combat these inefficiencies in the supply chain there is emerging a new style of relationship between the entities in the chain based upon a more open sharing of information. Instead of supply chain members having to anticipate requirements on the basis of forecasts, the aim now is to become *demand driven*. In other words, decisions on manufacture and delivery are taken in the light of knowledge of real requirement as far down the pipeline as it is possible to look. This is the basis for what has now come to be known as quick response logistics or, in the retail sector, more commonly termed efficient consumer response (ECR). The underlying principle of quick response is that information on actual sales or usage is transmitted back to the supplier in as close to real time as possible. The extension of the idea is that the information is also shared simultaneously with the supplier's supplier and so on. On the basis of this information each party in the chain can plan production, assembly, distribution and other activities so that a more efficient use of resources is achieved. In other words better use of production and transportation capacity is achieved whilst at the same time finished inventory and working capital is reduced dramatically.

"the aim now is to become demand driven"

The origins of quick response can be traced to the recognition by the apparel industry in the USA that it could not rely on protectionist legislation and appeals to consumers' patriotism to protect itself from low-cost competition from the Far East and other offshore competitors. Instead it had to look at how it could reduce dramatically the cost burden caused by the inefficient supply chain processes that permeated the industry. A study carried out by Kurt Salmon Associates reported that the US apparel supply chain, from raw material to consumer purchase, was 66 weeks. Of this, 11 weeks was in-plant time (fibre, textiles and apparel), 40 weeks was in warehouses or in transit (fibre, textile, apparel and retail), and 15 weeks was in-store. The report concluded that 'this long supply chain was both expensive to finance and, even more significantly, resulted in major losses as either too much or too little product was produced and distributed based on inaccurate forecasts of future demand'.

Banding together with Milliken

In 1981 US textile and apparel producers enjoyed an 80 per cent share of their domestic market. Six years later, their share was 60 per cent. Protectionist legislation slowed this decline, but profits went in to free fall, plunging from $1.9 billion in 1987 to $600 million in 1991.[1]

Searching for a competitive advantage, US industry leaders appealed to the patriotism of American consumers, forming the 'Crafted with Pride in the USA Council Inc.'. The council's 500 members funded a $100 million advertising programme to promote American-made clothing, but discovered that when it came to value-for-money clothing, American consumers were not that patriotic. Their next reaction was for the stronger parties in a supply chain to shift the burden of inventory to weaker players. This did not work either, because the disconnected and often adversarial supply chains were still slow, costly and ineffective.

Beyond the style-setting international couturiers, the critical success factors in the apparel industry are the ability to spot what will sell and then to get it into the shops first. In both respects, the US-based manufacturers were losing out badly to the likes of Italian fashion group Benetton, and the Far Eastern suppliers of phenomenally successful niche retailers like The Limited and The Gap. The council realized that efficiency and consumer responsiveness were the industry's best defence. The indigenous apparel industry could not compete on labour costs, but distance was in its favour. It should be able to compete in its own market by virtue of location, on time and transport costs.

In 1986 the council commissioned consultants Kurt Salmon Associates to study US apparel industry supply chains. The results were alarming. The supply chains were too long and too badly coordinated to respond effectively to market-place demands. Time to market averaged one and a quarter years from textile loom to store rack. Industry-wide the cost of this inefficiency was estimated to be approximately $25 billion per year, around 20 per cent of the industry's total turnover.[2] The supply chain could not absorb these costs, so they had been passed on to the customer – until imports became a threat.

The US industry had to find new ways of working if it was going to survive. Several pilot studies were therefore commissioned to see if pipelines could be shortened by collaboration between retailers, apparel manufactures and textile producers. Among the first to participate in the pilot studies was Milliken & Co., the country's largest textile producer.

Milliken's performance before embarking on the experiment was as follows: Milliken received incoming orders – slowly – by US mail. Weaving would normally be completed eight weeks after the yarn became available. Dyeing and finishing took a further four to five weeks. The stock would then be forwarded to the central warehouse until required by the customer. Throughput times were around 18–20 weeks from receipt of order. Keeping the factory operating at maximum capacity was the over-riding priority.

After Milliken, an apparel manufacturer could take around 18–20 weeks from receipt of cloth to get the clothing to a retailer.[3] The retailers, fearing stockouts, regularly over ordered, increasing their carrying costs and resulting in markdowns of excess stock. If the retailer's inventories got too high, then they would cut back on purchasing, leaving the manufacturers with excess stock. They in turn would cancel fabric orders, leaving Milliken holding unwanted inventory at its own cost.

In the pilot study, Milliken partnered with apparel manufacturer Seminole, and Wal-Mart stores. Consultants monitored a single product line (basic slacks), measuring the sales and profit improvement delivered by the implementation of quick response. The results showed increased sales of 31 per cent and a 30 per cent improvement in inventory turns.[4]

The exercise taught Milliken to look beyond its immediate customer – the apparel producer who paid the fabric invoice – so as to be responsive to the end consumers' requirements. If point-of-sale information could be shared between the partners, long-range forecasting and overstocking and order cancellations would no longer be necessary. Milliken began seeking out like-minded supply-chain partners who were willing to set aside short-term self-interest to create integrated supply chains.

The lessons learned in the apparel industry were used to improve other areas of Milliken's textile business. For example, the company approached one of its customers, a retailer of oriental-style rugs, with an offer to manufacture the rugs to order by quick response, then ship them by UPS direct to the customer's home. The retailer would, however, have to forward its customer orders to Milliken on a daily basis, and keep it fully informed of planned promotional activity. The retailer hesitated at first, but then agreed. The move allowed the retailer to eliminate its entire inventory of the product, keeping only display items, while cutting delivery times and costs because the rugs no longer passed through its distribution centre.

References

1 Konrad, Walecia (1992) Why Leslie Wexner Shops Overseas, *Business Week*, 3 February, p. 33.

2 Stalk, George Jr and Thomas M. Hout (1990) *Competing Against Time*, Free Press, New York, p. 249.
3 Harvard Business School (1993) Time Based Competition, Harvard Business School Management Programmes (video). Programme 2.
4 Stalk, George Jr and Thomas M. Hout (1990) *Competing Against Time*, Free Press, New York, p. 252.

A number of industry-wide initiatives in the US apparel business have led to increasing supply chain collaboration in order to speed up the flow of information through the chain and hence its responsiveness. Essentially what has happened is that information from the retail check-out counter through electronic point of sale (EPOS) data is transmitted back to the apparel manufacturer and from there to the upstream fabric maker and beyond that to the fibre manufacturer. Figure 4.5 summarizes the process.

It is clear that information technology plays a significant role in making quick response possible. However, it should be seen more as an enabler rather than a primary driver. The real pre-requisite for quick response is a re-orientation of the supply chain towards cooperation through shared information. A major study conducted in the European grocery retailing industry by a consortium of manufacturers and retailers led by Coca-Cola found that the adoption of quick response principles based upon the sharing of sales

"The pre-requisite for quick response is a re-orientation of the supply chain towards cooperation through shared information"

Smooth, continuous, demand driven product flow

Primary manufacture	Secondary manufacture	Tertiary manufacture	Retail outlet
• FIBRES e.g. Dupont	• FABRIC e.g. Milliken	• GARMENT e.g. Leslie Fay	• MERCHANDISE e.g. Dillards

Timely, accurate, paperless information flow

Two way flow of information
Product flow

Figure 4.5 Quick response in the US apparel industry. *Source*: Kurt Salmon Associates

data from the point of sale could lead to cost savings that translated into an additional profit opportunity of between 2.3 and 3.4 percentage points of sales turnover at retail prices. These benefits would be split between retailers (approximately 60 per cent) and suppliers (approximately 40 per cent). Paradoxically, even though the potential prize is so great, European retailers – with rare exceptions – have been slow to share point of sale data direct with manufacturers. Well-documented examples of supplier/retailer collaboration such as Wal-Mart's pioneering development of direct information links with suppliers through satellite-based electronic data interchange (EDI) are as yet not widely emulated in other Western retail markets.

Substituting information for inventory

BhS, a subsidiary of the Storehouse Group, is one of the largest high street retailers in the UK. Its 142 stores specialize in clothes for the modern woman and her family, decorative home furnishings, gifts and speciality packaged food. Since 1990, BhS has worked to refine its replenishment systems to the point where the effective use of information has all but eliminated the need to hold inventory.

As long ago as the early 1980s, BhS (then British Homes Stores) recognized that the unfolding IT revolution could deliver significant improvements in its logistics performance. Nevertheless it was to take several years – and the longest recession in retail history – before the potential benefits of harnessing IT across the entire supply chain were realized.

BhS had risen to the demands of the hectic 1980s with the installation of an early EPOS system, which significantly improved the quality of sales data available to store managers. For the first time managers could identify sales trends almost as they emerged. This advance meant that the lengthy replenishment process could be activated without delay, allowing BhS to maintain high service levels in the face of increasing consumer demand.

However, with the advent of recession, BhS was one of many high street fashion retailers to experience a chilling of the retail climate. Customers suddenly became more discerning, more value conscious, and much less prone to impulse buying. Profits plummeted.

In response, incoming chairman and chief executive, David Dworkin, commissioned a wide-ranging added-value analysis of all aspects of BhS's operations, including a major review of logistics, in November 1989. The review revealed that the benefits of improved replenishment had been at least partially negated by rising levels of obsolescent stock. The buoyant conditions of the 1980s had allowed bad stock management practices to flourish. In the stores, slow moving stock was marked down at the end of a season, but if it didn't sell, then it was marked back up again and offered for sale the following year. Consequently, some stores regularly refused to accept incoming deliveries of new merchandise because their store rooms were overflowing with unsold stock, some of it up to four years old. The practice was wholly supported by inappropriate accounting assumptions which appeared to make stock more, rather than less, valuable with age.

The operational review was completed, and in May 1990, BhS announced that it had decided to concentrate on its core competencies of buying and selling, outsourcing all other aspects of its operations to specialist contractors. With their help BhS went on to overhaul its stock management systems, and embrace the principles of quick response. A radical rework of the retailer's supply chain followed, leading to the abandonment of over half of its 800 suppliers. Only those that were willing and able to adapt to the demanding requirements of a long-term retailer–supplier relationship were retained. In the stores, the EPOS system was upgraded, and improved co-ordination of the buying function led to a more coherent and harmonious product range. The costly bulging stock rooms rapidly gave way to a system where almost all stock is held by suppliers, the majority of whom are EDI linked to BhS. By August 1991, an estimated 85 per cent of BhS's merchandise was called through the replenishment system by EDI. Plans were in place to lift the figure to 100 per cent. The EDI links gave BhS's suppliers access to data on how their own lines are selling in the stores, allowing them to detect emerging sales trends and anticipate replenishment orders. Goods could now be prepared and ready to ship by the time BhS called them through the pipeline.

A single specialist contractor, Exel Logistics, was appointed to handle the distribution of all of BhS's 8000 non-food and 350 food lines. Exel transports the merchandise – ready barcoded for its final destination – from suppliers to a single dedicated warehouse at Atherstone, Warwickshire, where it is sorted and despatched within 24 hours to BhS's UK stores. The daily deliveries arrive at the shops at between 6am and

10am each morning, just in time to meet the lunch-time shopping rush.

In five years BhS's replenishment cycles have been reduced to the point where 60 per cent of all orders arrive the next day and the full 100 per cent are released within 48 hours. The daily deliveries have reduced storage space requirements on BhS retail sites from 20 per cent to 10 per cent over the last 10 years. The company anticipates that further reductions will be possible at new retail sites.

Closely related to the idea of quick response (QR) and its retail version efficient consumer response (ECR) is the emerging concept of vendor managed inventory (VMI).

VMI is a planning process through which the supplier manages the flow of product into the customer's manufacturing or logistics system. This flow is triggered by frequent EDI information about the actual off-take or usage of the product at the level of the customer. With this information the supplier is able to take account of current inventories at each level in the chain as well as goods in-transit in determining what quantity to ship and when to ship it. The supplier is in effect managing the customer's inventory on his behalf. In a VMI environment there are no customer orders. Instead the supplier makes decisions on shipping quantities based upon the information they receive direct from the point of use or the point of sale. The supplier can also use this information to forecast future requirements and hence to better utilize his own production and logistics capacity.

"VMI is a planning process through which the supplier manages the flow of product into the customer's manufacturing or logistics system"

A number of industries are now moving towards the adoption of VMI. In the European petro-chemical industry for example, suppliers are using remote monitoring of customer inventories of certain bulk liquid products and are thus able to identify when replenishment delivery needs to be made. Similarly, petrol suppliers to retail petrol stations can now monitor remotely the sales of each grade of petrol and plan their deliveries accordingly.

In the USA the use of VMI in the packaged consumer goods retail business is widespread. Companies like Cheseborough-Ponds manage the inventories of major customers like K-Mart and report dramatic improvements in stock-turns on the retail shelf with fewer stock-outs. At the same time Cheseborough-

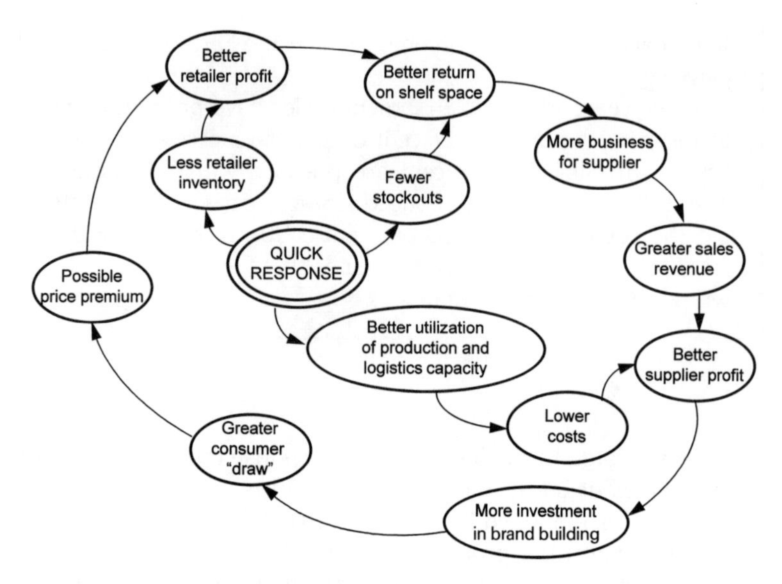

Figure 4.6 Creating a virtuous circle through quick response

Ponds benefit from earlier warning of requirements enabling them better to schedule production and delivery. Procter & Gamble report significant improvements in retailer stock-turn on their products where they operate in a VMI environment – stock-turns of 100+ on the retail shelf are not usual. At the same time they are using EPOS data to plan their own production and their own material requirements with their suppliers. The information highway for these companies is already a reality.

One further benefit of VMI to the customer is that it can be extended into the payment system. Thus the customer, in this regime, will only pay for the product after they use it or sell it. Hence the impact on their cash flow can be dramatic.

Quick response logistics generally has multiple benefits across the supply chain. Figure 4.6 suggests that quick response can lower suppliers' costs and so enable them to invest more in building the brand through innovation and classic marketing. If effective, such a programme can even justify a price premium. At the same time the customer benefits through lower inventory with few stock-outs. If the customer is a retailer or distributor they will also achieve a better return on shelf space and thus will be induced to give more business to the supplier. In other words a virtuous circle is created with continuing benefits to both the supplier and the customer.

Shifting the order penetration point

Capturing information on the requirements of customers or consumers as close as possible to the point of sale or point of use should be a key goal of supply chain management. However, for many organizations they are forced to anticipate those requirements through a forecast since they have no clear view of the final market place. Thus the supplier of packaging material to a chocolate manufacturer may not see anything other than the orders he receives from the chocolate company. Similarly the chocolate company will probably not see the real consumer demand off the shelf at the retailer, if the retailer only sends sporadic orders. In most supply chains the majority of manufacturing and distribution activities are driven by a forecast rather than by demand.

"many organizations are forced to anticipate those requirements through a forecast since they have no clear view of the final market place"

The point at which activities cease to be forecast driven and become demand driven is termed the 'order penetration point' although the term 'demand penetration point' might be more accurate.

Figure 4.7 shows different situations ranging from a 'make to order' environment, where demand penetrates to the far end of the chain to the more commonly encountered situation where only the last party in the chain interfacing with the consumer actually experiences real demand. All the activities upstream of the order penetration point are forecast driven with all the consequent problems that that can bring.

The challenge to the supply chain is to find ways in which the order penetration point can be pushed as far upstream as possible. At the same time a search for greater flexibility in manufacturing and logistics can contribute to an ability to carry inventory in a more generic or unfinished form – to be converted to its final form only when actual demand is identified. So, for example, Rank Xerox endeavour not to hold any product as fully finished inventory. Instead they will carry inventory as 'work in progress', in modular, semi-finished form and will then configure the final product only when an order is received. The benefit of this concept of 'postponement' is that less inventory is required and that it is 'generic' so the risk of over-stocking or, indeed, under-stocking, is reduced. At the same time customer service and choice is enhanced.

"The challenge to the supply chain is to find ways in which the order penetration point can be pushed as far upstream as possible"

In complex supply chains the only way that the order penetration point can be moved upstream is through collaboration

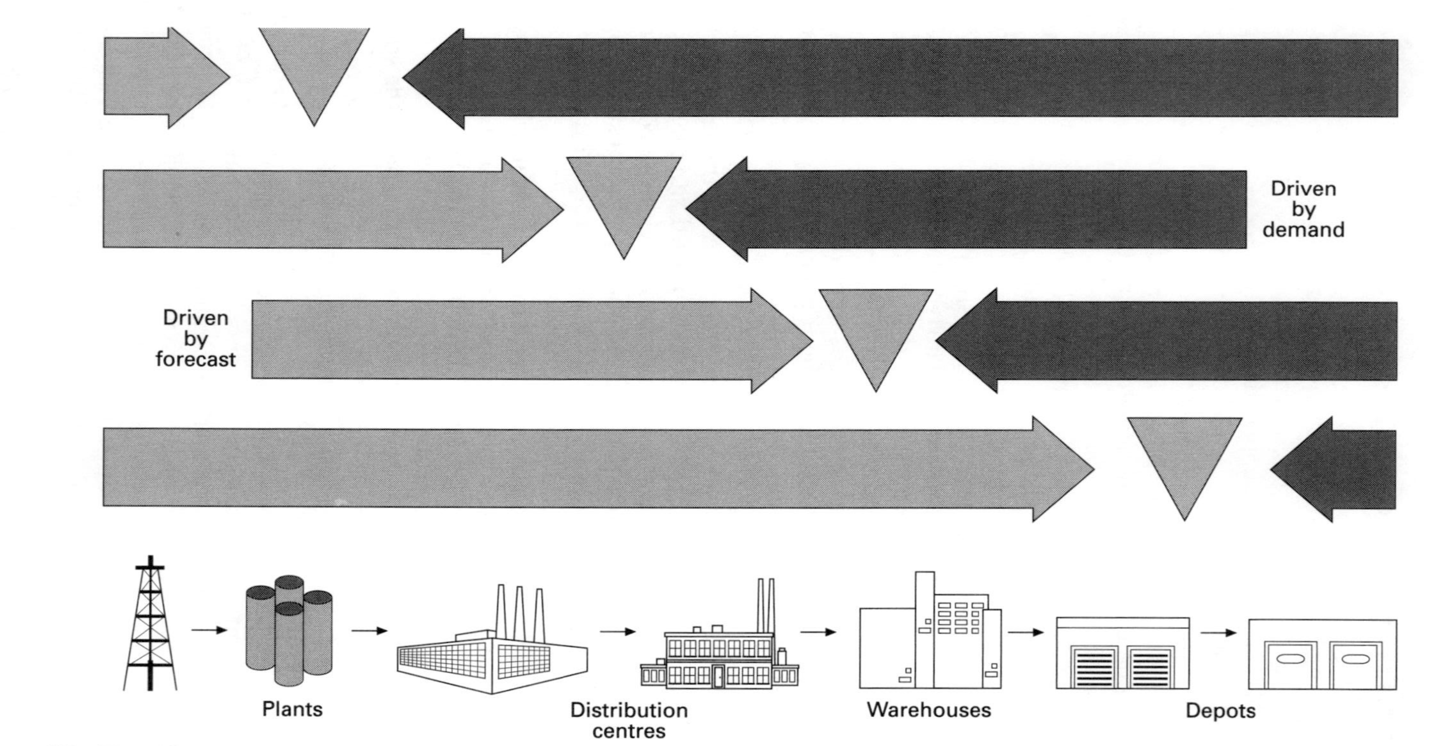

Figure 4.7 The order penetration point

between supply chain partners and, in particular, collaboration through the sharing of information.

The chapter began with the suggestion that there is a new concept of competition emerging in the form of what might be described as 'network competition'. It is based upon the principle that competitive advantage is achieved not just through traditional marketing strategies but by the cost-effectiveness of the supply chain as a whole. A fundamental element of competitive supply chain, we have suggested, is the way in which they share information and create greater customer value at less cost as a result.

Chapter checklist The move to supply chain management: key issues

- The emergence of the network organization
  - Focus on core competencies in the value chain
  - The rise of the 'boundary-less' business
  - Growing inter-dependency amongst supply chain members

- Partnership sourcing replaces adversarial relationships
  - Reduction in the supplier base
  - Open-book accountancy
  - The value-added exchange of information

- Creating 'lean' supply chains
  - Eliminating inventory buffers between parties in the chain
  - The arrival of the 'quick response' philosophy
  - The impact of vendor managed inventory on supply chain relations

CHAPTER 5

Time-based competition

In recent years, one of the most significant developments in the way that companies manage their operations and formulate their competitive strategies has been the focus on *time*. There are clearly many ways in which firms compete and through which they seek to gain advantage over their rivals. However, the ability to move quickly, whether it be in new product development or in replenishing customers' inventories, is increasingly recognized as a pre-requisite for market-place success.

The late twentieth century has seen the emergence of the *time-sensitive* customer. These time-sensitive customers can be found in every type of market, be it in high-tech markets where short life-cycles demand short lead-times, or in consumer durable manufacturing where just-in-time assembly requires just-in-time deliveries, or in everyday living where the pressures of managing a more complex, hectic life-style have led us to seek convenience – be it in banking, shopping or eating.

Whole industries have grown up around time compression, from overnight delivery to fast food. Technology has facilitated this process: cellular telephones, fax and satellite communications have all contributed to the continued search for the achievement of quicker response to the demands that customers place upon us. Now, quality is measured not just in terms of product performance but delivery performance as well. Few industries have been immune from these pressures and managers must constantly seek ever-more innovative ways of squeezing time out of every business process. Indeed, the main driver behind the business process re-engineering (BPR) philosophy has been the search for more time-effective ways of doing things.

Time reduction does not only lead to faster response to customer needs but, just as importantly, can lead to cost reduction and greater flexibility. In the previous chapter, an analogy was drawn with an oil pipeline. The longer the pipeline from, say a refinery to a distant market place, the slower it will be to respond to a change in demand in that market place. At the same time, the longer the pipeline the more oil is contained within it – hence the greater the working capital that is locked up. 'Time is money' may be a cliché, but in today's competitive market place it has never been more true.

" 'Time is money' may be a cliché, but in today's competitive market place it has never been more true"

Lack of responsiveness in logistics processes can heighten the risks both of stock-outs and thus lost sales, and over-stocked situations leading to mark-downs or stock write-offs. Compaq, the personal computer company, acknowledged that in 1994 their inability to respond to an upsurge in demand for their range of notebook computers led to estimated sales losses of up to $1 billion dollars. At the same time, Apple Computers were reported to have been forced to scrap 30,000 brand new Newton personal organizers because of an over-estimate of demand. Similar examples can be found in industries as diverse as clothing and electrical components.

The cash-to-cash cycle

In any business a critical measure of performance is the 'cash-to-cash' cycle. Put very simply this is a measure of the total cash that is locked up in the 'pipeline' from when materials or components are purchased from suppliers to when the finished product is sold and the cash received from customers.

One of the surprising features of the cash-to-cash cycle is just how long that cycle can be for many companies. It is not unusual to find pipelines within a business that are six months or more in length. Even more surprising is the fact that so many companies fail to measure, and hence to manage, these pipelines.

'End-to-end' pipeline time reflects all the stages of the logistics process including procurement lead-times, in-bound transit time, time spent in manufacturing, assembly and internal operations, order processing times, delivery times and, of course, time spent when nothing is happening and materials, work-in-progress and finished goods are 'sitting still' as inventory. Figure 5.1 highlights the ways in which time in the pipeline builds up.

It must be remembered that every day spent in the pipeline represents a cost to the business. Quite apart from the cost of funding the working capital employed there is the 'opportunity cost'. In other words whilst cash is locked up in the pipeline it cannot be put to use elsewhere in the business, or, indeed, invested elsewhere. In large organizations where a day's sales can be measured in millions of pounds or dollars then the cost of even an extra day of pipeline time will be considerable.

Taking time out of the pipeline will bring with it many benefits including:

- A one-off release of capital.
- A continuing benefit through the reduced cost of financing a shorter pipeline.
- Shorter response times, hence higher service levels.
- Less vulnerability to market-place volatility.
- More flexibility in meeting precise customer requirements, e.g. options, pack sizes, colours, etc.

Figure 5.2 demonstrates, at a generalized level, the effect that reducing pipeline time can have on profitability. The upward sloping line shows the cumulative build-up of cost from one end of the pipeline to the other. If time in the pipeline can be compressed then it is likely that both the fixed and variable costs can be reduced as the cost profile is 'shrunk'. The final result is greater profit per unit with the possibility, in a time-sensitive market, of greater sales.

There are three dimensions to time-based competition which must be managed in a coherent and integrated way if the organization is to become more agile and responsive – and hence more profitable:

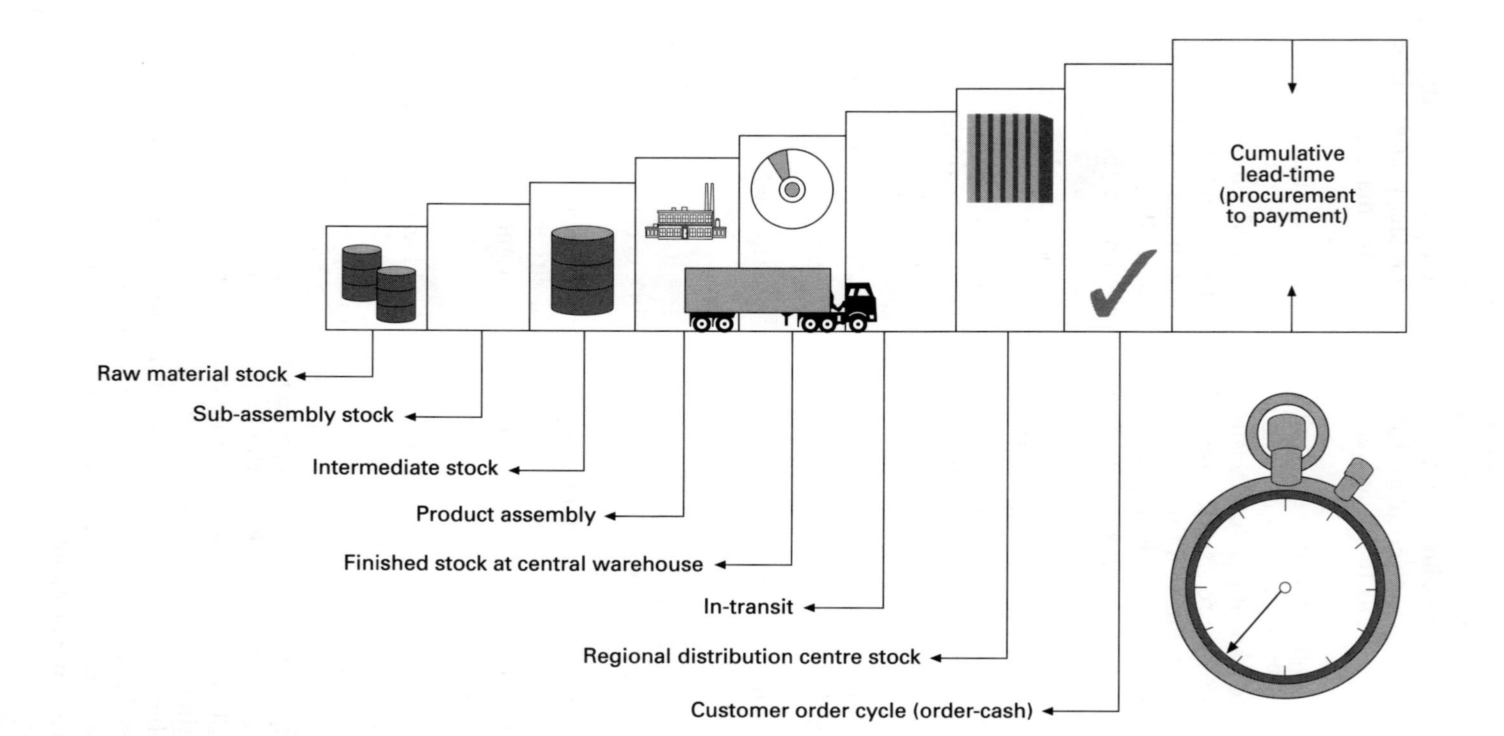

Figure 5.1 How long is the logistics pipeline?

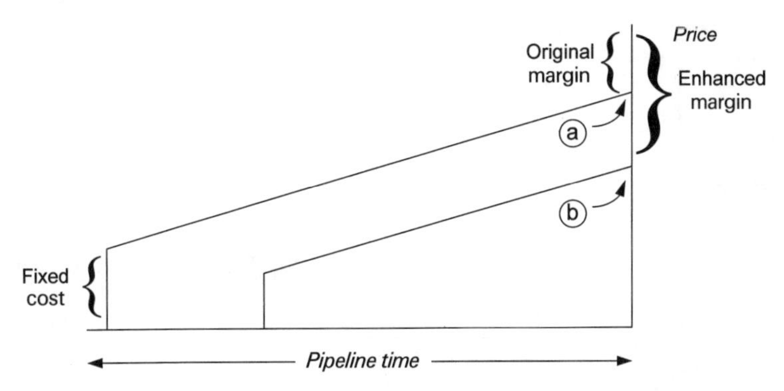

Figure 5.2 The impact of pipeline time on profit. (a) Cumulative costs before pipeline reduction; (b) cumulative costs after pipeline reduction

Time to market	How long does it take the business to recognize a market opportunity and to translate this into a product or service and to bring it to the market?
Time to serve	How long does it take to capture a customer's order and to deliver or install the product to the customer's satisfaction?
Time to react	How long does it take to adjust the output of the business in response to volatile demand? Can the 'tap' be turned on or off quickly?

Time to market

Innovation and timely new product development is a vital source of competitive advantage in any market. This has always been the case but it is made all the more necessary as a result of shortening product life-cycles. The product life-cycle represents the growth and decline in demand for a specific product in a particular market. Whilst it is rare for these life-cycles to be smooth and predictable one feature seems to be common across most industries and technologies and that is that these life cycles are getting shorter.

"life cycles are getting shorter"

In some cases technology change radically shortens the saleable life of a product. The personal computer market provides a classic example of this, to the extent that life cycles for some products are 12 months or less. In other cases changes in consumer taste, fashion or competitive pressures lead to rapid obsolescence or a switch in consumer preference.

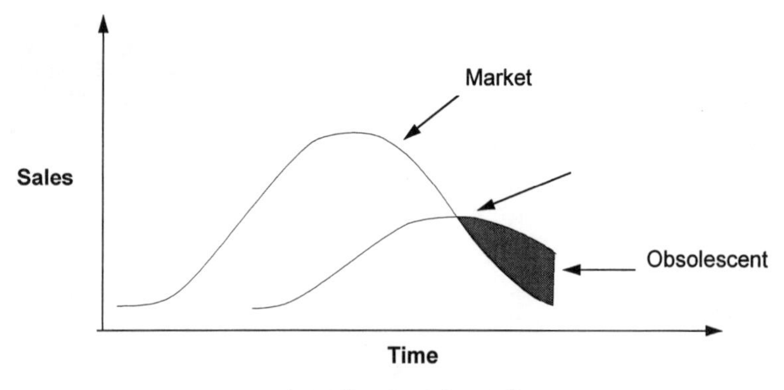

Figure 5.3 Shorter life-cycles make timing crucial

These shortening life-cycles make timing critical. Figure 5.3 highlights the double jeopardy facing companies that are slow to respond to market-place changes. In the first instance a late entrant will miss a sales opportunity that may well be captured by competitors. In the second case the company might find that just as its shipments into the market are getting up to speed, demand is already falling away – perhaps in response to the arrival of the next technology or competitive offer. As a result the likelihood is that the company will be left with obsolete or out-dated inventory resulting in mark-downs or even write-offs.

" 'Market understanding' is a pre-requisite for innovation"

One of the keys to speeding up time to market is the ability to be as close to the customer as possible. Continuous customer contact as a source of innovation is not a new idea, but is not always practised. Whilst many companies indulge in ad hoc market research few companies recognize the need to monitor customer and market trends on an on-going basis. 'Market understanding' is a pre-requisite for innovation – if we are slow to read the market it doesn't matter how quick we are in product design and manufacturing.

This type of continuous market research also implies a willingness to gauge customer reactions from the moment the product hits the market and to be prepared to modify the product as many times as may be necessary. Japanese consumer electronic companies such as Sony tend to be particularly good at making changes on the run. It has been suggested that rather than using the traditional Western approach to product design and development, which might be thought of as ready, aim, fire, the Japanese instead go for a concept of ready, fire, aim!

What this means is that because they have focused on flexibility and speed they are able to launch products, almost at prototype stage and then quickly modify them in the light of customer response.

Accelerating time to market – The Limited

The Limited is a Columbus, Ohio based apparel retailer that, during the 1980s, changed the face of fashion retailing in the US. Years before its competitors, The Limited developed computer controlled global supply chains honed to detect and exploit new fashion trends with breathtaking speed and efficiency.

The business was the brain child of entrepreneur Leslie Wexner, a young law-school drop-out who turned his back on a legal career to work with his parents in the family clothing store. The prevailing wisdom of the late 1950s stated that a clothing store should carry a full range of merchandise, offering its customers something for every occasion. The more expensive items such as women's suits and dresses carried the highest margins, and were therefore deemed to be the most profitable lines. Wexner disagreed, believing that the fashionable and lower priced sports wear was more profitable because it sold quickly. An examination of the books and the application of some basic cost accounting confirmed his suspicions that inventory costs made all the difference.

In 1963, Wexner quit the family business to open his own clothing store named 'The Limited' to reflect the fact that the store carried only a limited range of moderately priced high-fashion sportswear. The venture was hugely successful. By the mid-1970s The Limited was a publicly quoted company with 100 stores. A period of exponential growth followed during the 1980s, allowing a further six-fold increase in the number of Limited stores, and the acquisition and development of a string of women's apparel chains. By 1987, these chains were responsible for 7 per cent of all women's clothing sales in the US.[1]

At the heart of The Limited success was Wexner's flair for formula merchandising, backed up by the group's well-polished procurement systems. The procurement process begins with the Limited's scouts, who continually comb the world for hot new fashion ideas. Images of their finds are flashed back via satellite links to the Columbus HQ, where they are promptly copied. Computer aided design techniques are applied to bring the cut, colour, and other details into line with North American tastes. Moments later, small pilot orders are dispatched to EDI-linked suppliers in the low-cost manufacturing centres of Asia. Using Hong Kong as a consolidation centre, the goods are air freighted direct to The Limited's distribution centre in Columbus, in four weekly shipments aboard a specially chartered 747 jumbo jet. The goods, ready labelled and price tagged for display, are sorted immediately then forwarded, within two to three days, by road and air to retail sites all over the US. The whole process takes approximately three to five weeks from order to in-store display.

First deliveries of new lines are forwarded to designated retail test sites. The sites are selected by sophisticated computer analysis systems, which identify the locations most likely to provide reliable data to predict how well a given item will sell nationally. The systems can also pinpoint the best days in the year to test new merchandise, as well as the optimum dates to order fabrics and start garment production. The test results are used to determine the exact colour and size mix of subsequent orders, reducing further the possibility of acquiring the wrong stock.

Mistakes do occur, but The Limited's systems deal with these just as decisively. Every item arrives in the store with its anticipated 'in stock' and 'out of stock' date already defined. Between the two are predetermined windows of opportunity for reorder or order cancellation, as well as progressive markdown schedules for slow moving stock. Old inventory is continuously marked down, rather than allowing it to remain in the stores waiting for large and late markdowns at the end of the season. As a result, The Limited achieves five to six inventory turns a year, compared to the speciality store average of three or four.[2]

References

1 Weiner, Steven B. (1987) The Unlimited?, *Forbes*, 6 April, pp. 76–80.
2 Aufreuter, Nora Nancy, Karch, Shi and Smith, Christiana (1993) The Engine of Success in Retailing, *McKinsey Quarterly*, No. 3, pp. 101–116.

However it takes more than a close contact with customers to reduce the time taken from the drawing board to the market.

It used to take from 10 to 15 years in the automobile industry to take an idea from concept to the dealer's showroom. Now companies like Rover can introduce new models in under two years. The secret is 'simultaneous' or 'parallel' engineering. Traditional product development was a sequential process characterized by a series of quite separate stages such as R&D, engineering, prototyping, marketing research and so on. Often ideas would get some way down the chain before it was realized that the concept needed revision in some way. So 'back to the drawing board' was a frequently encountered cry.

Now the best companies create self-managed, multidisciplinary teams who are given the authority to take whatever actions are necessary to bring the product to market. So, for example, companies like 3M will bring research scientists, production specialists, market researchers and logistics managers together and encourage them to work as a team to solve problems and to work in 'parallel'. Not only is time significantly compressed through this approach but problems are more readily identified and solved.

Bringing logistics management into the new product development process can prove beneficial. For example if product design decisions can take account of transport and storage requirements then significant improvements to lifetime profits might result. Again, having logistics management involved early in the design process may well lead to the identification of potential problems if components or packaging materials with long replenishment lead-times are being considered. Often product modifications made at the design stage can have significant effects on total pipeline time once the product is commercialized because materials and components with long replenishment lead-times are avoided.

"Bringing logistics management into the new product development process can prove beneficial"

Time to serve

'Time to serve' can be defined as the elapsed time from the initiation of an order by a customer to the final delivery or installation. Inevitably, in a time-sensitive world shorter order cycles can provide significant competitive advantage. Closely coupled with the demands from customers for shorter delivery lead-times is the requirement for *reliability*. In an environment

"in a time-sensitive world shorter order cycles can provide significant competitive advantage"

where more organizations are seeking to minimize their inventories and manage on a 'just-in-time' basis, suppliers must be able to guarantee delivery times – even down to time windows as narrow as an hour.

Managing the order-to-delivery cycle requires an understanding of the order fulfilment process and the causes of time consumption and variability within it. The goal should be to seek to simplify and streamline what can often be an unnecessarily complex sequence of activities, performed usually one after the other in a linear manner. Re-engineering the order fulfilment process to reduce time consumption and variability involves a fundamental review of the way that orders are captured, credit is controlled, production is scheduled and transport is planned. The following four-step procedure can be used to advantage:

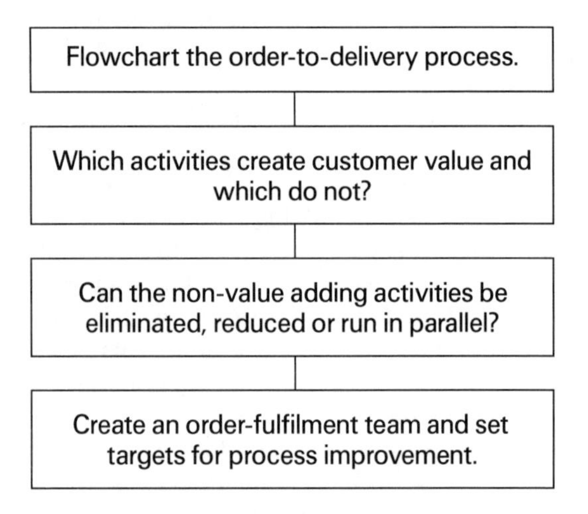

Flow-charting the order-to-delivery process in detail should be the starting point of a time compression programme. Somehow or another, over the years, most companies have created amazingly complex processes for converting a customer's order into cash. These extensive processes have been further institutionalized through computerization. Managers are often surprised to be confronted with the results of a flow-charting exercise on, say, order processing. 'Something as simple as processing an order surely cannot involve over 100 separate steps', would be a not-untypical response.

To simplify and speed up the order-to-delivery cycle requires a cross-functional approach. A powerful way to achieve significant improvements in this crucial area is through the creation of an order fulfilment team which draws from all the functional activities involved in the chain of events from receipt of order through to final delivery and invoicing. Thus sales order entry, credit control, production planning, transport scheduling and invoicing are all represented on the team. The first priority of the team is to focus on ways in which the entire process can be simplified through the elimination of activities or by running those activities in parallel rather than in series, by reducing paperwork and reports and by questioning the conventional wisdom of how the business should be run.

Invariably this type of cross-functional analysis will reveal many ways in which order-to-delivery times can be improved. Because these re-engineered systems will often be simpler, they will normally be cheaper to operate and will require fewer people to run them.

The order fulfilment team should also form the vehicle for the on-going processing of orders once the systems have been simplified. In other words instead of the traditional means of processing orders where the order moves from one department to another, there should be an order-fulfilment group working as a cross-functional team to manage the order on an integrated basis, from the capture of that order to the final delivery of the product.

Time to react

Volatile markets have become the norm in so many industry sectors. Significant upward and downward changes in demand occur almost unpredictably. Many of these swings are due to competitive actions, some are due to changes in customer taste or fashion and some are self inflicted as the result of promotional activity or the like.

"Volatile markets have become the norm in many industry sectors"

Managing logistics in these conditions is not easy and the likelihood of stock-outs, or conversely overstocks increases. A response so often heard from managers faced with circumstances such as these is: 'if only we had better forecasts'. The reality is that forecasting technology is as good now as it probably ever will be and in any case nothing short of a crystal ball will predict short-term demand in wildly fluctuating markets. The real challenge is to seek ways in which we can become less dependent upon the forecast.

Karrimor: rapid response in a seasonal market

Karrimor International Ltd is a family controlled manufacturer of rucksacks and specialist clothing for climbers and hikers. Founded in 1946, in the small town of Accrington in the north of England, Karrimor started out as a manufacturer of cycle bags, but in 1957 switched its focus to rucksacks. During the 1960s and 1970s, close links with leading mountaineers enabled Karrimor to develop its world-renowned range of rugged and well engineered climbers' rucksacks. But by the 1980s, the company's future looked anything but secure. It was becoming increasingly difficult to protect Karrimor's technological innovations – and its market share – from a host of me-too competitors.

Realizing the danger, Tony Parsons, son of the company's founders Charles and Mary Parsons, began to look for ways to improve Karrimor's competitive position. Joining the British branch of an American businessman's club, gave Parsons an opportunity to visit other enterprises, and learn from their experience. One in particular, Milliken, the North American textile giant, left a lasting impression. The speed at which Milliken was able to produce goods to order amazed Parsons, and although his own business was tiny by comparison, he realized that it too could gain considerable advantage by improving its response times.

With the help of a newly appointed outsider, Tony Cameron, Parsons set about devising a plan to revitalize the business. First, Karrimor was to be the most responsive supplier in its market. Second, it would produce a range of patentable products to stave off the me-too competition. Third, it would introduce a counter-seasonal garment range to even out cash flow and inventory levels. Finally, it would sell off the old buildings it currently occupied and move to a purpose-built leasehold property nearby. The great advantage of the latter would be that product flows were no longer hampered by production taking place on several floors. Moreover, it would dramatically improve communication between the production and marketing functions, who were presently located in separate buildings.

New equipment was installed, and once the workforce had fully settled into the new site, Parsons began channelling his energies into the development of the new garment range. Meanwhile, two new directors were appointed and charged with improving the company's response times and customer relations, and with streamlining the shop floor.

Karrimor and its retailers both suffered from deliveries that were heavily skewed towards the start of the season. Retailers took their entire stock then, which meant that Karrimor had to build to stock ahead of time or attempt to cram as much production as possible through a short delivery window. Instead Karrimor decided to introduce a simple form of quick response, inviting retailers to place only a small trial order at the beginning of the season. This would be delivered in the normal way, with a tear-off label attached to each item. When an item is sold, the retailer simply returns (or faxes), the label back to Karrimor, specifying the quantity required, either a single replacement, or several if the item is selling well.

Retailers were initially reluctant to adopt the system, despite its benefits and simplicity. Larger retailers were unwilling to try new ways of working, and smaller ones looked to them for a lead. In the end a trial was negotiated with a 15-outlet chain of stores, committing Karrimor to a 21-day delivery response. The trial was an immediate success, and by 1993, 370 outlets were using the stockflow system which by then handled over 75 per cent of sales. This paved the way for Karrimor's new garment range, speeding market penetration by minimizing the risk associated with a brand extension for both supplier and retailer.

Karrimor's manufacturing systems were forced to change as more and more business was called through on quick response. Work-in-progress throughput times were reduced by replacing the factory's piecework payment system with a method that was more conducive to small batch work, and less time consuming to administer.

Sourcing was the next issue to be addressed. A 'supplier day' was held to explain the changes that Karrimor was undertaking. This was quite a departure for a company operating in such a traditional corner of the textile industry, but Karrimor was eager to develop quick-response purchasing to support the quick-response sales and manufacturing systems it had already introduced. Some suppliers responded well to the call for smaller, more frequent and more reliable deliveries, but where necessary, unresponsive suppliers were replaced. A local supplier of rucksack fabric installed new dyeing vessels, allowing it to produce dyed fabric in smaller batches with faster lead-times. The improved supplier response times allowed Karrimor to change its production planning process. Orders for undyed fabric could be placed with the supplier, but the colour need not be confirmed until a later date. If one colour is selling better than another, suppliers' manufacturing schedules can be switched to accommodate demand. Better still, Karrimor can advise retailers to reconsider if they had ordered items in one colour, while another colour was enjoying twice the stockturn.

Source: Based on 'Karrimor Accrington', a case study by Malcolm Wheatley, Colin New and Jeremy Watts, *Management Today* Best Factory Awards: *Management Today*/Cranfield School of Management, 1993

The reason why so much logistics activity is forecast-dependent is because of long lead-times. The longer the lead-time the further ahead we need to forecast. Lead-times here refer to the time it takes us to respond to an upward or a downward change in demand. If we have long replenishment lead-times for raw materials or packaging supplies, for example, of necessity we are forced to try to forecast demand over that lead-time.

"The reason why so much logistics activity is forecast-dependent is because of long lead-times"

The problem is that forecast accuracy tends to vary directly with lead-times. The longer the lead-time the greater the forecast error, indeed the error tends to increase more than proportionately the further ahead we have to forecast and, of course, forecast error is one of the major determinants of the need for safety stock. Figure 5.4 shows the effect of lead-times on forecast error. One rule of thumb suggests that reducing the lead-time by 50 per cent will reduce forecast error by 50 per cent.

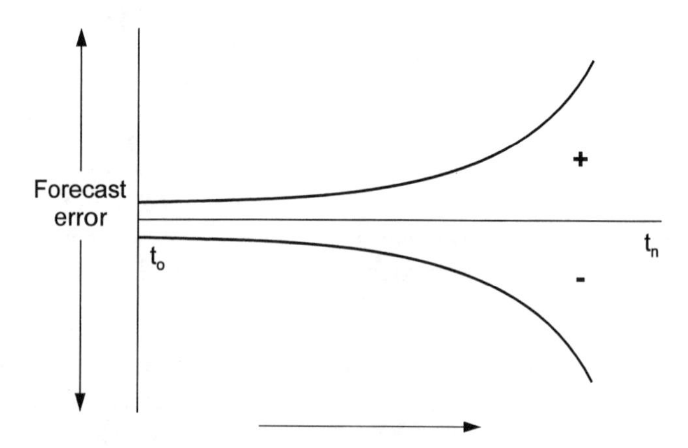

Figure 5.4 Forecast error and lead-time

With the trend towards the globalization of industry, lead-times if anything have tended to lengthen. Off-shore manufacturing or sourcing may reduce the costs of manufacture but it can often lead to longer pipelines with higher levels of variability in total end-to-end time. A further compounding element is that with complex products containing many components or materials it is the speed of the slowest moving element that determines total pipeline time.

One international brewing company found that the forecast horizon for its West African operation was three months long. Not because it took that long to brew the beer but because the gold foil that went on top of the bottle could not be sourced locally and had to be procured through their European buying organization – with a three month lead-time! Not only did this necessitate a three-month forecast of demand for the product but it also limits flexibility of response. For example, if for some unexpected reason demand for beer rose then the ability to meet that increased demand would be severely impaired.

Many companies have invested great sums in manufacturing automation to speed up throughput times in the factory but find that because the pipeline as a whole is inflexible they still have problems reacting to demand changes. For example, best practice in the Western European car industry has reduced the time taken to assemble a car to 24 hours. Yet average inventory of finished products – cars waiting to be sold – is still in the region of two months for many companies. Hence the ability of these companies to meet the precise needs of customers for specific models and options is constrained.

What in practice can be done to reduce lead-times in a business so that it might simultaneously improve delivery performance and reaction times?

Strategies for lead-time reduction

From the earlier discussion it will be clear that a number of significant benefits can be gained if pipeline time can be reduced. Not only does lead-time reduction free up working capital but it can also enable faster and more flexible response.

The key to unlocking these prizes lies in what might be termed *strategic lead-time management*. To manage lead-times strategically requires an understanding of their character. For most products there will not be one lead-time but many, as each component that goes into the final product may be subject to different lead-times as they move from different suppliers through different supply chains. For most purposes however it is sensible to take the slowest moving element in the chain to determine total pipeline length. It is almost like *critical path analysis* in that attempts to shorten pipeline time should proceed by working to reduce that longest lead-time until some other element emerges as the critical path and so on.

To assist us in the identification of opportunities for pipeline reduction it will be helpful to 'map' the pipeline from one end to the other. A pipeline or supply chain map is essentially a time-based representation of the processes that are involved as the materials or products move through the chain. At the same time the map should show the time that is consumed when those materials or products are simply standing still, i.e. as inventory.

In these maps it is usual to distinguish between 'horizontal' time and 'vertical' time. Horizontal time is time spent in process. It could be in-transit time, manufacturing or assembly time, order-processing time and so on. It may not necessarily be time when customer value is being created but at least something is going on. The other type of time is vertical time, this is time when nothing is happening and hence the material or product is standing still as inventory. No value is being added during vertical time, only cost.

The labels 'horizontal' and 'vertical' refer to the maps themselves where the two axes reflect process time and time spent as static inventory respectively. Figure 5.5 depicts such a map of the manufacture and distribution of men's underwear.

From this map it can be seen that horizontal time is 60 days. In other words the various processes of gathering materials, spinning, knitting, dyeing, finishing, sewing and so on, take 60 days to complete from start to finish. This is important because horizontal time determines the time that it would take the system to respond to an increase in demand. Hence if there was a sudden upsurge in demand it would take that long to 'ramp-up' output to the new level. Conversely if there was a downturn in demand then the critical measure is pipeline volume, i.e. the sum of both horizontal and vertical time. In other words it would take 175 days to 'drain' the system of inventory. So in volatile fashion markets, for instance, pipeline volume is a critical determinant of business risk.

Pipeline maps can also provide a useful internal benchmark. Because each day of process time requires a day of inventory to 'cover' that day then, in an 'ideal' world, the only inventory would be that needed to provide cover during the process

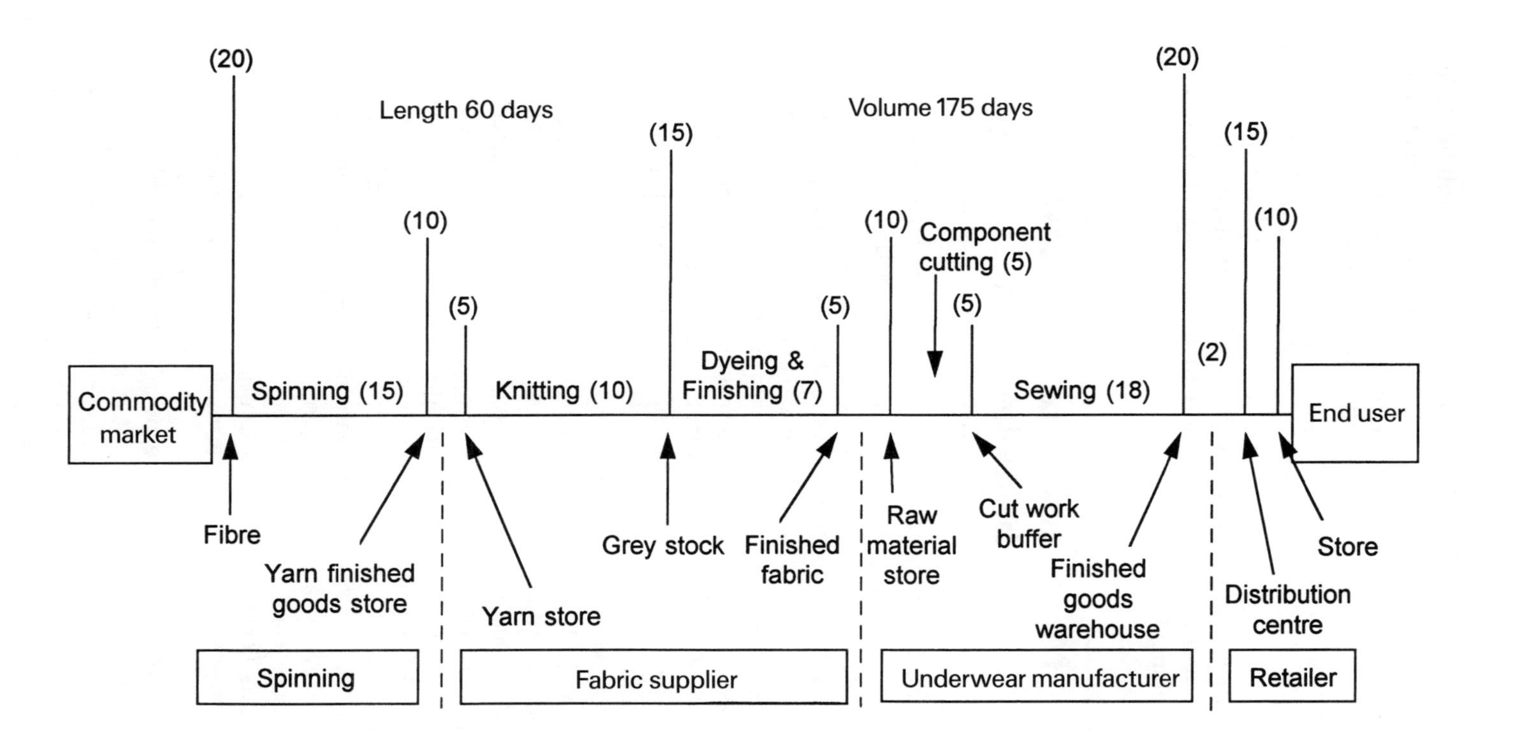

Figure 5.5 Supply chain management – an example. *Source*: Scott, Charles & Roy Westbrook (1991) New Strategic Tools for Supply Chain Management, *International Journal of Physical Distribution and Logistics Management*, **21**, No. 1

lead-time. So a 60-day total process time would result in 60 days inventory. However, in the case highlighted here there are actually 175 days of inventory in the pipeline. Clearly, unless the individual processes are highly time-variable, there is more inventory than can be justified.

Mapping pipelines in this way provides a powerful basis for logistics re-engineering projects. Because we have made the total process and its associated inventory transparent, we are now in a much better position to identify opportunities for improvement.

Mass customization: Levi's bespoke jeans

In 1853, a tailor named Levi Strauss set up business in San Francisco, making blue denim jeans. The business prospered. In time, tailoring gave way to mass production, and Levi Strauss & Co. grew to become the world's largest clothing manufacturer. For almost one and a half centuries, the quality of the products and the strength of the Levi Strauss brand were enough to guarantee a market for Levi's jeans. But by the late 1980s intensified competition and ever more demanding retailers had put the issue of customer service high on the management agenda.

From the early 1990s the company invested in more responsive and efficient manufacturing and supply systems. In its US factories, relatively inflexible assembly lines were replaced with self-managing teams, using leading-edge manufacturing and communications technology. The new manufacturing systems reduced lead-times and inventory, while Levi's retailer inventory management system 'LeviLink' improved product availability, replenishment, and overall standards of service. The company's capabilities were enhanced to such an extent that Levi Strauss could again offer individually made-to-measure jeans.

Levi's 'Perfect Pair' service provides female customers with custom-made tapered-leg jeans, for only a few dollars more than off-the-peg alternatives. The company already offered its mass-produced standard jeans in over 170 women's, junior and petite, sizes and fits, but the introduction of Perfect Pair aimed to cater for its most discerning denim buyers. The service was launched in the US and Canada through selected Levi stores, where customers' measurements are taken by specially trained sales assistants, then fed into a computer terminal. Using specially designed software, the system identifies a code number for an appropriate pair of trial jeans, which the customer tries on. Minor deviations in size and shape are recorded, and when the customer is totally satisfied with the fit, details of the order are forwarded by modem to a Levi's factory in Tennessee. There a dedicated team make up the Perfect Pair, for delivery within three weeks. The customer's details are retained on computer by Levi, and a bar code displaying the customer reference number is sewn into the waistband of each Perfect Pair. The customer can then contact Levi's at any time, and quoting her bar-code number, order additional pairs of jeans in a range of colours and finishes.

The introduction of the 'Perfect Pair' was heralded by industry analysts as a major breakthrough in customer service, and sent sales soaring by up to 300 per cent at early test sites. Made-to-measure products still account for only a tiny percentage of Levi Strauss's business, but some industry observers believe that bespoke products will become an everyday feature of the electronic shopping malls.

Value-added time/ non-value-added time

One of the reasons that logistics pipelines tend to be longer than is justified by the actual manufacturing and transportation time is because so much time is consumed in what we term *non-value-adding* activities. These are activities which, if a way could be found to reduce the time spent on them, or even to eliminate them, then there would be no noticeable reduction in value from the customer's perspective. If for example we reduced the time taken to process an order then the customer would not see this as a reduction in value, indeed if it meant they got the delivery sooner they might regard it as an improvement. Likewise a reduction of inventory in a warehouse as long as it did not lead to more out-of-stock situations, would not reduce customer value although it would most certainly reduce costs.

A good starting point therefore for time compression projects is to analyse the pipeline from start to finish classifying every step in the chain in terms of whether customer value is being created at that step or merely cost. It can be quite depressing to perform these analyses and to discover that only a small

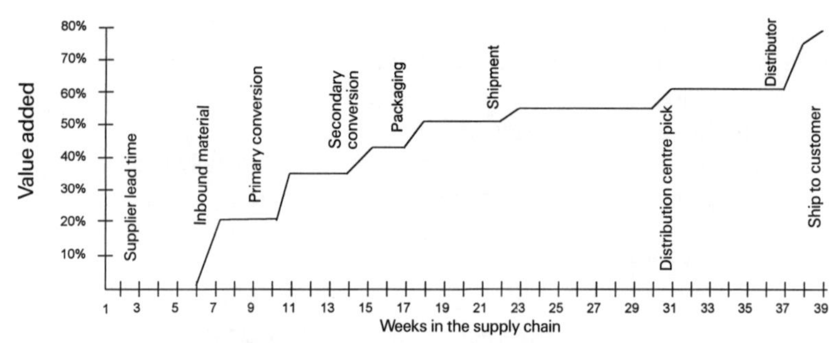

Figure 5.6 Value added through time

proportion of time in the pipeline is actually spent creating customer value. Figure 5.6 gives an actual example from the pharmaceutical industry.

This is not an extreme case. It is quite common to encounter organizations where less than 10 per cent of total pipeline time is consumed in creating customer value. If anything, the problem has been exacerbated by modern manufacturing technology where automation enables products to be manufactured in ever-shorter time frames and in greater volumes – but only to sit as finished inventory in a warehouse waiting for demand to catch up with production.

"The real focus of logistics process re-engineering should be upon finding ways to reduce the non-value-adding components of total pipeline time"

The real focus of logistics process re-engineering should be upon finding ways to reduce the non-value-adding components of total pipeline time. Clearly there may be cost implications which will need to be weighed in the balance, but more often than not speeding up processes actually leads to significant overall cost reduction as well as to a reduction in total system inventory.

The three stages of time

The brief but fast history of time-based competition indicates that companies that have become successful practitioners of the strategy have moved through three phases. In phase one, management discovers the power of time, either intentionally or unintentionally. The discovery may come about as a competitive emergency, a response to an unanticipated threat from a competitor, or an isolated experiment in a factory that is looking to solve a particular problem.

For example, a plant management team facing quality problems and out-of-control inventories may apply just-in-time methods to its factory to address these nagging issues, and remarkably, both improve. As an unexpected bonus, the managers also discover that they can deliver on customer orders much faster.

At first, the sales force may not notice the factory's new speed or be very interested in it – until a customer sends out an urgent call for quick delivery of a product. With its new time-based approach, the factory responds, and this time the sales force notices. Then the whole organization proceeds to stage two of time-based competition.

In stage two, the organization as a whole discovers the power of time to unleash innovation. Everything that can be done faster is done faster; champions emerge in every part of the company to re-engineer every process. The company compresses its billing processes, its order-to-quote and order-to-delivery cycles. The enthusiasm spills over to engineering and marketing; the new product development and introduction processes are compressed.

At one level, the results are heroic. The company is faster, leaner, sharper. Time compression yields impressive cost reductions and quality improvements. Perhaps most important, it frees up valuable human and capital resources. Some of these resources can be claimed as improved profits; but in most companies, innovation becomes an addiction. Braced by their new-found ability to run faster and harder, companies cannot resist the impulse to push it to the limit.

This is precisely the path that Japanese companies took to their own ruin. Innovation becomes an end in itself. The capabilities of time-based competitors enable them to produce smaller and smaller gradations of innovation, launched faster and faster into the market. To the company, it feels as if it is making the most of its ability to innovate and get to the market fast. In reality, the company is squandering its resources. It may launch more varieties of a product, but it fails to invest the time and energy to look for new ways to do business with customers that will take full advantage of newly enhanced or created capabilities.

In stage three, companies alter their momentum. They stop simply doing everything faster and put speed and innovation to work in the service of the customer. They apply the discipline of the market place and build the skill of their employees to create competitive advantage. The key to stage three is focus: companies that master the capabilities of the first two stages now bring them to bear in an integrated system that focuses on understanding the needs of customers and the capabilities of competitors, segmenting customers by their sensitivity to time, prioritizing improvement efforts within the company and linking the company's success to that of its key customers. Management must provide focus by constantly asking the questions that tie the needs of customers to the capabilities of processes to create identifiable and exploitable competitive advantage.

Source: George Stalk, Jr and Alan M. Webber, Japan's Dark Side of Time, *Harvard Business Review*, July-August 1993

Logistics process re-engineering

There has been a tendency by some to see business process re-engineering (BPR) as yet another management fad with a focus primarily on cost and overhead reduction. This is a pity since the philosophy of BPR, which essentially is about simplification and the reduction of non-value-adding activities, has much to offer organizations seeking to become more responsive to customer demand.

Many logistics systems – order processing for example – have developed in a haphazard and organic way in response to circumstances of history. As the business grew in size it might well have taken on more people in its order entry department. These people then required more supervisors who had to file more reports. Similarly as the business grew with new accounts being gained, changes to the credit control function were made to routinize the activity. Inevitably this added to the complexity of the process. Then as further products were added to the range the problems of production planning and scheduling grew, so formalized planning systems were installed. Now we have a business with multiple systems and procedures which do not always fit well together and where inevitably the amount of time involved from start to finish has increased considerably.

The challenge to logistics process re-engineering is to find ways to reduce the complexity of these systems and to simplify them. Automation and technology have greatly assisted in the speeding up of logistics processes, but not necessarily their simplification. In many cases we have simply computerized existing inefficiencies in our systems.

Elsewhere in the logistics system opportunities for time compression can be found through eliminating stages in a multi-echelon distribution chain. Many companies, particularly in overseas distribution, have traditionally moved inventory from factory through regional distribution centres to national warehouses and even to local stocking points. The original logic for this arrangement was that transport costs could be minimized by shipping in bulk and that distant markets could maintain inventory to cover against long transit times.

Today's logic might argue much more strongly for making use of direct delivery wherever possible. Intermediate stock holding rarely if ever adds customer value (only if some form of break-bulk activity, packaging or final configuration is involved). Eliminating these steps will reduce total system inventory, handling and warehouse costs and will of course reduce lead-times. Whilst transportation costs might increase, the overall benefit from both a service and a cost point of view will be positive.

"Today's logic might argue much more strongly for making use of direct delivery wherever possible"

Re-engineering the flow of information from the market place to the supplier and beyond can have a profound effect on responsiveness. As we have observed in Chapter 4, improving the visibility of real demand right the way back through the supply chain enables each party in that chain to better anticipate demand. At the moment too much information on demand is hidden by intermediate inventories in the form of distribution centres and warehouses. Even though those stocking points may be essential to the efficient physical flow of product, they should not be allowed to act as filters of information on real demand. Likewise when orders are transmitted back from one stage in the chain to another, great benefit could be gained if the order could distinguish between that part of it which is to replenish depleted inventory and that part which reflects an increase in real demand.

Speeding up the flow of information and relating it more directly to real movements in market place demand can do more to enable a business to become a time-based competitor than almost anything else. Because most companies have a 'lead-time gap', that is the total pipeline time is greater than the customer's willingness to wait, then information must be used to close the gap. If not then the system will become dependent upon inventory to service customers, with all the attendant problems that brings. Figure 5.7 illustrates the lead-time gap.

"Speeding up the flow of information can enable a business to become a time-based competitor"

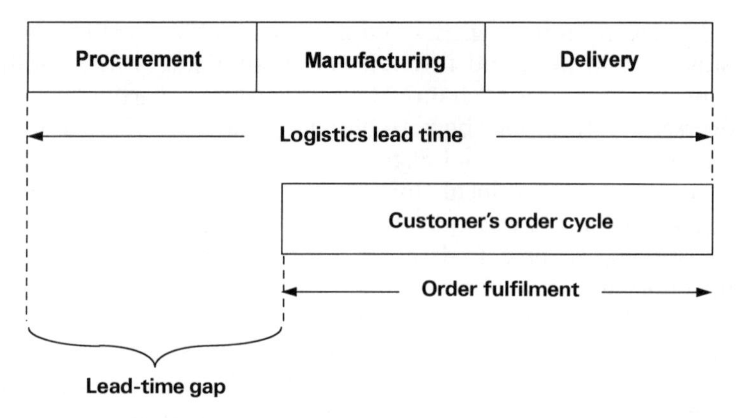

Figure 5.7 The lead-time gap

The key to reducing the lead-time gap lies not only in reducing total pipeline time but also in gaining earlier warning of customer requirements. The latter is achieved through establishing better communication with customers and, ideally, by getting as close as possible to 'real-time' demand. In other words if what is happening in the final market place could be communicated as far as possible up the supply chain – as it happens – then all parties in that chain could move much closer to just-in-time response. As we discussed in Chapter 4, there are significant advantages to be gained from sharing information through the marketing channel, even if there may be reluctance to do so.

Time-based competition is now widely accepted as a powerful basis for gaining advantage in volatile markets and in an environment where product life-cycles are shortening. Not every product or every market requires a just-in-time strategy and the costs of time compression may not always justify the benefits. However, the more demanding the customer becomes and the more the competitive pressure intensifies, then almost inevitably the prizes will go to the more responsive organization.

Chapter checklist Time-based competition: key issues

- Time becomes a critical source of competitive advantage
  - Reducing time to market, time to serve and time to react
  - The planning horizon and forecast error
  - Shorter pipelines provide greater flexibility at less cost

- Strategies for lead-time reduction
  - Understanding total pipeline time
  - Pipeline mapping as a means of focusing improvement activities
  - The difference between value-adding time and non-value-adding time

- Logistics process re-engineering
  - Understand and simplify logistics processes
  - Measure and manage the 'lead-time gap'
  - Substitute information and responsiveness for inventory

CHAPTER 6

Serving the global customer

One of the most striking trends in recent years has been the rapid increase in the globalization of markets. Not only is this true in the case of well-established brands like Coca-Cola, Marlboro or Gucci, but it is also apparent in markets as diverse as computing, automobiles and consumer electronics. Nor is the trend to globalization confined only to products; we see similar transformations in services whether it be banking, retailing or satellite TV.

At the same time, the corporations that have created and developed these global brands are re-focusing their operations so that they too are global in their scope. What this means is that an electronics company, for example, may source some if its components in one country, sub-assemble in another with final assembly taking place in a third country. Managing these complex global networks becomes one of the prime challenges to the achievement of profitability.

There is an increasing tendency for organizations to source materials, assemble and manufacture items off-shore. The motivation for this is largely economic, based upon the search for cost reduction. These cost savings may be available through lower labour rates, lower costs of material, lower taxes, lower costs of capital or greater government assistance. At the same time, these organizations may also rationalize production so that individual country operations no longer produce a full range of products for their own national markets. Instead, the company may now focus production on fewer factories which make a limited range of items but for a regional or even global market. The opportunities for enhanced economies of scale in production through such strategies may be considerable. However, at the same time, the logistical challenges presented by these global networks are significant.

For many years now the trend towards the globalization of industry and of markets has been apparent. Commentators have suggested that as industries seek ever greater economies of scale and as global brands continue to develop, the need to develop transnational business strategies will become ever more pressing. The global business is distinguished not only by its search for wider markets for its products, but by the tendency to source its materials and components on a worldwide basis and to manufacture in whatever off-shore locations provide optimum costs. Inevitably such companies will have a heightened need to co-ordinate a far more complex network of flows of materials, products and information than would be the case with the more traditional nationally-based company. Hence the challenge to the global business will increasingly be seen as logistical, i.e. how to integrate and manage the mesh of interconnections between suppliers, factories, distribution centres and customers.

"the challenge to the global business will increasingly be seen as logistical"

The logic of the global corporation is clear: it seeks to grow its business by extending its markets, whilst at the same time seeking cost reduction through scale economies in purchasing and production and through focused manufacturing and/or assembly operations.

However, whilst the logic of globalization is strong, we must recognize that it also presents certain challenges. First, world markets are not homogeneous, there is still a requirement for local variation in many product categories. Second, unless there is a high level of co-ordination, the complex logistics of managing global supply chains may result in higher costs.

These two challenges are related: on the one hand, how to offer local markets the variety they seek whilst still gaining the

"There is a danger that some global companies in their search for cost advantage may take too narrow a view of cost"

advantage of standardized global production, and on the other, how to manage the links in the global chain from sources of supply through to end user. There is a danger that some global companies in their search for cost advantage may take too narrow a view of cost and only see the cost reduction that may be achieved by the focusing of production. In reality it is a total cost trade-off where the costs of longer supply pipelines may sometimes outweigh the production cost saving.

Many issues are raised by the spread of globalization. Concerns have been expressed about the impact of the growth of out-sourcing and off-shore manufacturing leading to the emergence of the 'hollow corporation' with the consequent implications for employment. Further questions arise concerning the apparent contradiction between the move to globalization with the potential risk of increased lead-times and the search for just-in-time, zero-inventory type strategies which require shorter, not longer, pipelines.

Developing a global logistics strategy

A number of issues arise when global logistics strategies are being considered. One key concern is the question of the appropriate degree of centralized direction as against local autonomy. Traditionally many companies have preferred to devolve decision-making to a local level. Yet, almost by definition it is difficult to see how global supply chains can be optimized in terms of service and cost if they are planned and managed on a fragmented, local basis. On the other hand the attractions of local autonomy are clear in terms of responsiveness to the market and the ability to 'stay close to the customer'.

A second, related, issue is the extent to which synergy can be released by global co-ordination and whether this is compatible with local decision-making in sourcing, production and distribution. Many global companies, for example, have sought to establish 'centres of excellence', particularly in R&D and in production, whereby resources and/or technologies are concentrated for greater focus. However, separating new product development and production from the market may not necessarily be sound practice, especially where those markets are not homogeneous.

Running in parallel with these two issues is the question of how the search for economies of scale in production and the benefits of standardization can be reconciled with the need to meet different local requirements and to do so with ever higher levels of responsiveness.

Each of these three issues has significant implications for the way in which logistics is positioned organizationally in the global business and each is examined in detail below:

(i) Centralization versus local autonomy

There is a widely held view that globalization implies centralization of management and control. However, whilst there are attractions to central planning and strategy formulation there is a basic conflict with the ever-present need to stay as close to local markets as possible. The Swedish/Swiss global business, ABB, under its chief executive, Percy Barnevik, has sought to bring these two potentially opposing ideas together under the slogan 'Think global, act local'. This is achieved at ABB by a matrix structure with strategic integration being achieved through a 12-person executive committee. Each committee member manages one of eight business segments – power plants, power transmission, power distribution, transportation, industry, environmental control, financial services and a miscellaneous segment called 'various activities' which embraces robotics and telecommunications – and/or a country or region. These managers and their businesses will be located wherever in the world the market suggests is most appropriate. The role of the centre is to collect, through a centralized reporting system, performance data on the company's 5000 profit centres and to use this information to manage total corporate resources. Individual businesses are run locally, but within a framework established centrally, so, for example, decisions on which market should be serviced from which factory would be centrally determined.

" 'Think global, act local' "

In the case of logistics planning the need for central decision making but with local implementation is equally strong. Many companies have gone beyond the centralization of decision-making to centralize production and distribution facilities. The concept of the 'focused factory' has taken hold – particularly in Europe – spurred on by the moves toward the single market.

Focused factories, as the name implies, concentrate on the production of a limited range of products often sharing a similar manufacturing process or technology. So whereas in the past companies might have factories in individual countries producing the full range of products for that country, now they might have fewer locations with each factory specializing in a unique product portfolio but producing them in greater volumes.

"An inevitable effect of focused factories is the greater complexity of transport and distribution"

An inevitable effect of focused factories is the greater complexity of transport and distribution: previously one factory served one market, now one factory serves multiple markets. Also, whilst substantial opportunities for economies of scale through centralized production may exist in many industries, there may also be the risk of longer lead-times and the loss of flexibility in meeting local customer needs. Because these local needs can be quite different (local language packaging, distinct tastes, specific service requirements and so on), it is essential that the global business does not confuse the need for centralized strategy determination and pipeline coordination with the overly simplistic idea that globalization is only about economies of scale in production.

"many organizations are now learning that it is possible to coordinate logistics centrally and yet meet local needs cost-effectively"

In fact many organizations are now learning that it is possible to coordinate logistics centrally and yet meet local needs cost-effectively. This is achieved through linking individual facilities, sales offices and supply sources through shared information. The concept now is one of 'distributed distribution'. What this in effect means is that we manage production and inventory as if it were centralized, but the actual physical location of production and inventories are determined by other factors – specifically the market and/or sources of supply. The idea of 'virtual' inventory is central to this approach. Virtual inventory is managed as if it were a single inventory – hence the total inventory in the system can be substantially reduced – yet it may be physically dispersed according to where it is most appropriate to hold it. SKF, through their global forecasting and supply system (GFSS) are able to manage demand across Europe through a single centre, allocate production to specific plants, schedule transport between plants and local trans-shipment points, and in so doing, dramatically improve customer service but with much reduced total inventory and better utilization of production capacity.

Virtual inventory and the square root rule

It has long been recognized that by reducing the number of stock locations and by consolidating inventory in fewer places, higher levels of service can be achieved with less total inventory.

This benefit is achieved through what might be termed 'risk pooling' so that demand variability in more than one market is covered by the same safety stock. The rule of thumb that generally applies in determining the reduction in total system inventory following a rationalization in the number of locations is called the 'square root rule'. This tells us that the reduction in inventory will be proportionate to the square root of the number of stock locations before and after the rationalization. Hence a reduction in worldwide stock locations from, say 100 to 25 would lead to a reduction in inventory of approximately 50 per cent, i.e. in the ratio of $\sqrt{100}$ to $\sqrt{25}$ or 10 : 5.

Interestingly, it is not actually necessary to *physically* reduce the number of stock locations to achieve the benefits of the square root rule. All that is required is that the inventory be managed as if it were one inventory – in other words to control it centrally. The idea behind *virtual inventory* is that the computer becomes the warehouse and that stock levels are determined centrally on the basis of total visibility of demand from all sources. The location of specific stock will be determined according to where it makes greatest sense to keep it.

It must also be recognized that whilst the inventory savings can be substantial through virtual inventory – in effect there is only one 'warehouse' – the costs of transport will usually be higher as product is moved greater distances in smaller quantities.

(ii) Achieving global synergies

The concept of synergy is simple. The whole should be more than the sum of the parts. Alternatively it is often described as the '2 + 2 = 5' effect. One of the main drivers of the trend towards the globalization of industry is the search for synergy, particularly in manufacturing and logistics.

It has often been suggested that there can be significant benefits if R&D, product development, manufacturing and marketing can be coordinated in order to avoid 're-inventing the wheel' country by country and also through economies of scale in procurement and production.

The Japanese have been very visible in their coordinated approach to world markets in industries such as automobiles, consumer electronics and machine tools. Even where they have established off-shore manufacturing such as their European 'transplant' factories, they still seek to ensure that they are managed within the framework of their worldwide strategy.

"opportunities exist for significant economies through centralized purchasing"

In areas such as procurement, opportunities exist for significant economies through centralized purchasing. Many multinational companies (i.e. companies with multiple local operations) incur considerable cost penalties because they source components, packaging material, transport and other services locally and independently.

Perhaps the biggest opportunity for global synergy lies in the co-ordination of the physical logistics system. If companies are organized nationally with a high level of local autonomy in logistics management then the likelihood is that there will be a cost penalty that can significantly erode profits. Hence the pressure that now exists in such companies to centralize the coordination of transportation and warehousing and to balance world-wide flows of product and inventory decisions.

A key area for the achievement of global synergy is through the use of global order management and information systems. With complete visibility of worldwide demand and supply, the organization can identify least-cost service options, e.g. which customers should be sourced from which location so as to achieve optimum production and transportation economies whilst minimizing inventory. Communications technology enables organizations, if they wish, to centralize order management and customer service through call centres where the customer only places a local call. Whilst many companies prefer to localize their customer liaison, e.g. local sales offices, there is no reason why at the same time order processing and management cannot be centralized.

(iii) Standardized yet customized

Whilst much has been written about the globalization of markets it would be wrong to assume that the world is ready for standard products. There are still considerable differences in local tastes, preferences and requirements. Language differences mean that packaging will often need to be specific to a country, local regulations may require product modification and so on.

"There are still considerable differences in local tastes, preferences and requirements"

All of this presents a significant challenge to the management of the global logistics system. For example, even a basic personal computer will need to be produced in different versions to take account of local voltage and plug type, and the keyboard and manuals will need to take account of the language of the user as might the software itself.

A number of issues are raised by the need to 'localize' products particularly in a production-oriented environment where the goal is more normally to seek unit cost reduction through the economies of scale, generated by producing a uniform product in volume. Specifically the questions to be answered are:

- Can the final configuration or assembly of the product be delayed until real demand is ascertained?
- At what level in the chain should inventory be held and where should final configuration take place?
- Where should the forecast be made – in the local market or at the centre?

The first issue concerns *postponement*. This is the fast-growing idea that suggests that where there is a demand for variety in the market place, products should not be finally configured until actual demand is known. Instead they are produced to a generic level, using common components or materials and are held as work-in-progress inventory (WIP) rather than finished goods inventory (FGI). Final configuration may take place locally or centrally depending upon the economics of production, transportation and packaging. By final configuration is meant the final assembly, finishing, kitting or packaging of the product.

One of the most frequently quoted examples of the postponement concept is provided by Benetton, the Italian fashion manufacturer and retailer. Whereas most manufacturers of, say, a red pullover would take some yarn, dye it red and then knit the red pullover, at Benetton they do it differently. There they take the plain, undyed yarn and knit a pullover. Garments can then be dyed in small batches when demand is known. The advantages of this are considerable. Firstly, only one colour is held in stock – plain, undyed, grey – thus dramatically reducing the amount of inventory held in total. Secondly, great flexibility is achieved since the garment can be dyed in any colour depending upon local demand. In a global fashion business with different seasons, trends and local preferences, this degree of flexibility provides a significant marketing edge.

Benetton's global logistics system

The Benetton Group is an integrated manufacturer and marketer of fashionable knitwear, casual clothing and accessories, based in the tiny village of Ponzano Veneto, in northern Italy. In less than 30 years, a unique combination of design flair, shrewd business acumen, and an understanding of supply chain management has propelled its development from cottage industry to Italy's largest clothing manufacturer. The group produces 80 million garments per year, but not a single item is produced for sale without a pre-placed order from one of the 7000 licensed Benetton stores dotted around the globe.

Benetton's retail network – comprising the United Colours of Benetton, Sisley and 012 chains – sell only the group's branded products, which are designed to appeal to an international target market of fashion conscious 15–24-year-olds. The universality of the stock is tempered by individual store managers, who adjust their own product mix to suit local tastes by selecting appropriate styles and colours.

For the store managers, the stock selection process begins seven months in advance of the two annual fashion seasons (spring/summer and autumn/winter). Each store must commit 80 per cent of the season's orders at this point. These are produced and shipped on a 20-day order cycle. The remaining 20 per cent of orders – resulting from forecast errors, surprise hot sellers, or small 'flash' collections – can be satisfied by quick response in 7–8 days. Each month has its own stock rotation, with 28 rotations per year for some goods, making it possible to have entirely new collections in the shops every few months. Since the early 1980s the orders themselves have been transmitted by EDI directly from the shops, or through one of the company's 85 regional agents, to Benetton's HQ.[1] This regular influx of orders and sales data provides Benetton with daily updates of demand and market conditions, enabling it to adjust manufacturing in line with demand.

Benetton's manufacturing operation is famed for its flexibility. Careful production planning allows it to produce the urgent 20 per cent of orders by quick response, while production of the remaining non-urgent 80 per cent can be scheduled to maximize its capacity utilization. However, only those operations (such as design, cutting, dying and packing), which enhance cost-efficiency through economies of scale, or are deemed essential to the maintenance of product quality, are performed in-house. All other manufacturing (including the labour intensive finishing stages), are completed by a local network of 200 suppliers and 850 subcontractors, most of which are small family businesses. All are closely tied into Benetton's manufacturing, information and logistics systems.

Logistics and process efficiency are considered at every stage of garment design and production. In the early 1970s Benetton recognized and exploited the benefits of postponement, dying small batches of finished knitwear to order, rather than knitting them from a pre-determined coloured yarn. More recently, the company has developed software for machine-knitted seamless sweaters, the benefit being that no hand finishing is required.[2]

Most of the 80 million garments produced annually by the group are distributed through its automated central warehouse, built (partially below ground) close to Ponzano, at Castrette di Villorba. The $50m computer-controlled facility is operated by a staff of 20 and handles 30,000 cartons per day. Underground passages link the warehouse to a nearby cotton garments plant and a high-tech cutting and packing facility. Goods enter the warehouse via conveyor belt from the adjoining factories, or through one of 50 receiving bays. Each of the (reusable) cartons are bar-coded before they enter the huge subterranean distribution complex, so they can be electronically sorted, then either held temporarily, or forwarded on for immediate shipment. Around 15,000 cartons are shipped each day from Castrette and most (approximately 70 per cent) are exported to Benetton stores in 109 other countries. Invoicing is completed at the warehouse, by transport staff, while the company's own in-house freight forwarder and customs broker prepare customs documents and consolidate shipments for sea and air. All documentation is sent by the customs broker via EDI to points of entry, so that goods are never delayed by missing paperwork. Half are air freighted on an eight-day order cycle time, others go by rail or sea, or a combination of both. For environmental reasons Benetton is moving away from road transport and, in 1995, was considering switching to night-time store deliveries to avoid city centre congestion.

Benetton's long-term investment in logistics efficiency has been repaid with the fastest cycle times in the industry, no excess work in progress, little residual stock to be liquidated at the end of the season, and near perfect customer service.[3]

References

1 Dapiran, Peter (1992) Benetton – Global Logistics in Action, *Asia Pacific International Journal of Business Logistics*, **4**, No. 3, pp. 7–11.
2 *The Economist* (1994) Benetton: The Next Era, 23 April, p. 92.
3 Foster, Thomas A. (1993) Global Logistics Benetton Style, *Distribution*, No. 10, October, pp. 62–66.

The second issue concerns the deployment and location of inventory. Conventional logistics systems have tended to be based around inventories of fully finished products being held in dispersed locations waiting to be sold. Today's logic of integrated supply chain management suggests that wherever possible inventory should be held in as few locations as possible, in as generic a form as possible to be localized or customized when real demand is identified.

Localizing generic products at Hewlett Packard

In an industry that is characterized by punishingly short product lifecycles and extreme unpredictability, getting the right products to the right market on time is an absolute imperative. For computer equipment manufacturer Hewlett Packard the need to manufacture and deliver its products quickly, reliably, and ever more cost effectively has led to the development of capabilities that put it at the very forefront of global supply chain management.

Product complexity was a hidden enemy for Hewlett Packard, for while the company served a global market place with seemingly global products, these products were almost always tailored to meet local specifications. They had to be delivered with power cords and transformers to meet the local voltage, and supplied with keyboards, manuals and operating software in the appropriate local language. This meant that instead of dealing with a single product line, produced and distributed to meet an overall global forecast, Hewlett Packard was producing differently configured machines to meet estimated demand in each of a number of relatively small markets. But the smaller the market, the more erratic the order patterns were likely to be, and the more difficult it was to predict demand accurately.

The uncertainty reverberated back through every stage of the supply chain, wrong footing internal and external suppliers alike, leading to exaggerated safety stocks, and increased risk from obsolete stock or of expensive reworking. There were, for example, five physically separate Hewlett Packard facilities contributing to the manufacture and distribution of its best-selling family of low-cost 'DeskJet' printers, resulting in a pipeline that was nearly six months long.

Supplying the European market with its tightly packed cluster of nations and linguistic differences was particularly troublesome, with huge safety stocks needed to meet Hewlett Packard's goal of 98 per cent service levels. Product mangers, while wishing to lessen their exposure to variability in the supply chain, were eager to reduce the amount of inventory in the system, freeing up cash for other uses. An investigation of how current service levels might be maintained at lower cost was therefore commissioned.

Under the then-current system, the printers were 'localized' at the central factory, leaving ready packaged for sale in the country of destination. Stockpiles of each of the different language variants were then held at regional distribution centres, ready to meet sudden fluctuations in demand. The question that quickly arose was what would be the value of switching production over to a single form of generic printer, with 'localization' postponed until the distribution centre stage, i.e. delaying the point of commitment until a firm order had been received.

Hewlett Packard had been honing its inventory network modelling skills for some time, and was therefore able to apply these skills to modelling the DeskJet supply chain. The results indicated that costs of safety stocks could be significantly reduced if a generic printer was introduced. First, safety stocks could be lowered from seven weeks of finished goods to around five weeks of the generic version, as fewer generic printers would be required to maintain service levels. Second, the cost of each unit stockpiled would be reduced because less value had been added by this point. Anticipated savings were in excess of $30 million per year, on current volumes. The costs associated with performing the localization process at the distribution centres were slightly higher than if performed by the factory, and higher overall stocks of localization materials would be required with the dispersal of this activity. Nevertheless, these costs were dwarfed by the overall savings on inventory. Furthermore, savings amounting to several million dollars per annum were also identified from reduced shipping costs. The generic printers could be packed more densely and therefore transported more cheaply than before.

The logic of switching to a generic printer for the European market was unimpeachable. The US market already had its own factory-produced version of the generic printer so, ostensibly, there seemed to be no case for extending the practice to the European market. Surely there could be no benefit in postponing completion for such a large and homogeneous market? Not so. An extension of the DeskJet study evaluated a proposal to factory-produce two versions of the printer, an ultra lost-cost US version and a generic one to serve the rest of the world. This proposal was rejected however, because of the potential strategic time advantage offered by a single generic printer strategy. The critical factor here was the increased unpredictability of even regional forecasts (for the Americas, Asia and Europe) when set against a forecast for overall global demand. If, contrary to all earlier indications, demand for a new product failed to materialize in, say the US, while in the rest of the world sales took off at an unprecedented rate, pipelines would already be filled to meet predicted demand. A generic printer strategy would allow the immediate diversion of stocks to wherever they were required, at minimal cost and with minimal delay and loss of service. Contrast this with the prospect of reworking unneeded stocks before redirection, or waiting until programmed output could meet demand. In a market with narrowing windows of opportunity, the risk of the latter was deemed to be too great. Hewlett Packard introduced its global generic printer.

Based on material contained in Davis, T. (1993) Effective Supply Chain Management, *Sloan Management Review*, Summer, pp. 35–46

In a multi-product environment the distribution of sales by stock-keeping unit (SKU) tends to conform to the Pareto rule, i.e. 80 per cent of the volume comes from just 20 per cent of the SKUs. This can be of considerable help when global logistics strategies are being devised. For example, the fastest moving lines (the 20 per cent that provide 80 per cent of the total volume) can be held as finished inventory because demand is likely to be more predictable. These lines can also be carried in local markets, having been shipped there in bulk so as to take advantage of production and transportation scale economies. Because they are fast movers stock-turn will be higher so in effect only a limited investment in inventory is required. These products should not move through intermediate stock locations such as regional distribution centres but should be delivered direct.

At the other extreme, the slow moving products may be held regionally or even centrally and, wherever possible, at a generic level to be finally configured when precise local requirements are known. Where the value/density of these products is high and/or their 'critical value' to customers is high (e.g. vital spares) then overnight delivery using Fedex, DHL or UPS type services may be appropriate.

"slow moving products may be held regionally or even centrally at a generic level to be finally configured when precise local requirements are known"

DHL helps Fujitsu enhance global service

Fujitsu Personal Systems (FPS) is a wholly owned subsidiary of Fujitsu with headquarters in California, USA. This division of Fujitsu produces hand-held computers, of the type used by sales people or service engineers. Manufacturing takes place in Japan, but markets are worldwide.

In order to service their European customers better, Fujitsu established a partnership with DHL. Products flow through the DHL Express Logistics Centre (ELC) in Brussels, Belgium, for overnight delivery to FPS's European customers. The ELC carries out incoming quality and functional inspection, kitting and configuration and repair. The ELC has a 400 square metre technical support facility with a full 'clean room' environment. Fully qualified technicians are employed by DHL having been trained by Fujitsu engineers and the facility is an approved Fujitsu repair centre. All work carried out in the centre carries the full Fujitsu warranty.

Kitting and configuration of products in the ELC enables Fujitsu to hold lower inventories for a given service level, as the ELC is able to customize the basic models and ship the same day. DHL now undertake all order processing and inventory management on behalf of FPS in Europe.

Spare computers are kept in the ELC as partly configured inventory. When a salesperson's machine breaks down in the field, the ELC is notified. A spare machine is plugged into the customer's global telecommunications network and receives a download of the appropriate database for that salesperson from the customer's mainframe computer in the USA. The ELC technician verifies that the machine functions correctly before it is packed and shipped for next day delivery to the salesperson.

Recently, DHL joined FPS in a joint sales presentation to a potential FPS customer. The customer was seeking a supplier of hand-held computers for its European sales force and gave the order to Fujitsu on the basis of its after-sales service capability (provided by DHL).

Figure 6.1 suggests some guidelines for the location of inventory in a global network based upon the volume and the predictability of the item. Using the 80/20 principle we can centralize the vast majority of the slow moving, less predictable lines achieving a considerable reduction in total inventory. Almost certainly the reduction in inventory carrying costs will more than compensate for the higher cost of express delivery.

The third of the issues referred to earlier is the question of where the forecast should be made. In one sense the closer to the point of final demand the better it is to forecast in order that local conditions can be factored into the equation.

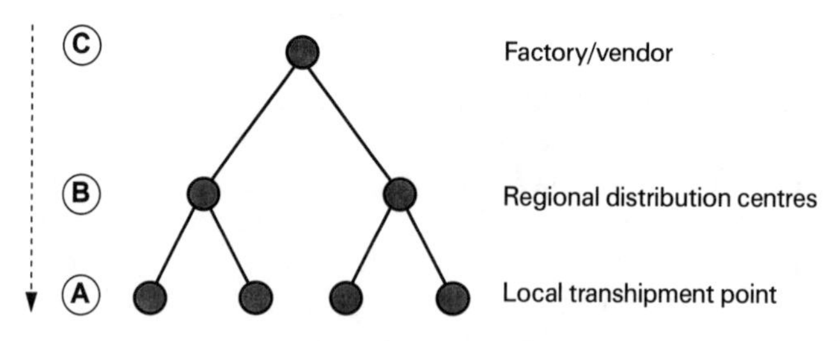

Key:

- Ⓐ Direct shipment of fast moving, predictable lines. Held locally, probably pre-configured
- Ⓑ Inventory of medium velocity, less predictable demand lines held at generic level awaiting final configuration
- Ⓒ Slowest moving lines, least predictable. Perhaps one shared global inventory or make to order.

Figure 6.1 Inventory location in a global network

However, these local forecasts will inevitably be prone to more error than an aggregate forecast made further up the chain.

In the case of Gillette reported below, it was found that it was better to forecast sales at a generic level (i.e. an aggregate European forecast) and to hold stock prior to localization (i.e. unpackaged). The same generic inventory can then be used to satisfy local demand with local language packaging, promotional packs or whatever.

Gillette's global logistics strategy

The Gillette company is a long-established company with a corporate brand name that is recognized world-wide. Its declared mission is to achieve leadership in the following categories: male grooming; male and female shaving and deodorants and anti-perspirants; writing instruments; dental care and small electrical appliances. The corporate strategy is to run the business on a global basis maximizing the power of Gillette's well established brands. To quote Alfred Zeien, the chairman of the company: 'We sell the same products world-wide ... we treat all markets the same ... when people shop they do not think very differently from Americans.' Even though there was still a recognition of local requirements and differences in demand, the intention was to build a global business around a common approach with respect to the development and marketing of Gillette products around the world.

However, despite the company's commitment to a global marketing strategy, there was a lack of integration of its logistics management – particularly across Europe. Responsibility for logistics was very fragmented with localized manufacture and distribution management. A European HQ had been established in London, England, but decisions on everything from inventory levels to purchasing decisions were made locally. There were 13 warehouses across Europe all carrying virtually identical stock, except that packaging varied locally.

Even allowing for all this inventory, service levels to retail customers were low. Order fill averaged only 78 per cent, and the order cycle time varied from five days to more than 20 days. Service performance was increasingly important as European retailers continued to grow their purchasing power and to place ever greater demands for service upon their suppliers.

Many of the markets in which Gillette competed were highly volatile with high levels of promotional activity requiring special promotional packs or over-wraps. In situations such as this, forecasting was difficult and consequently there was always great pressure placed upon manufacturing to make frequent changes to its production schedules. Manufacturing worked on a monthly planning cycle and hence needed to have reliable forecasts to cover the planning period as well as any extended lead-times required by suppliers.

It seemed inevitable that if the company wanted to develop further its global approach to marketing, it would need to underpin this with a greater degree of central coordination and planning. A European logistics strategy required a number of fundamental decisions to be made at a European level rather than locally. In particular responsibility for inventory management and forecasting would need to be centralized.

The centralization of responsibility for finished goods inventory necessitated the establishment of a European planning function. The task of the function was to obtain sales forecasts from each local market, monitor finished goods' stock levels at each warehouse and develop production plans and stock movement schedules to drive the flow of finished goods to warehouse to ensure a high service level. Although, in retrospect, this seems a logical move, there was a great deal of resistance by local business managers to the centralization of responsibility for what they saw as their stock of finished goods. The belief was widespread that service levels would suffer as inventory levels were pushed down.

By 1990 the company was ready to move to the next stage of sophistication in planning. Up to this point all planning had been done in monthly buckets, with the consequence that stocks were still at a high level, although service had improved dramatically. Since a Europe-wide forecasting system had been installed it had become clear that they could forecast overall European demand centrally much more accurately than they could by adding up all the local sales forecasts. This led to the implementation of weekly planning, backed-up by capacity-constrained master scheduling. The essence of this is that basic factory operations, namely the production of blades and razors, are driven by accurate, stable European forecasts while the more volatile packaging requirements are driven by national, item-level forecasts. Differences between the two are buffered by work-in-process inventory which, in turn, required the centralization of its responsibility. Although, in reality, there is close partnership between European and factory planning teams, the centralization of control over work-in-process has been a major step forward, not only at the European level, but also across the North Atlantic business.

A major contribution to integrated materials management was made in 1991 when responsibility for all purchasing was centralized. This did not mean that purchasing teams within the factories were disbanded, merely that they now reported to a central executive with a brief to act locally but think North Atlantic. The benefits of this to the company have been the significant reductions in purchase prices achieved. Gillette are currently standardizing purchasing systems and working on a number of projects to reduce inventories of raw material and work-in-process which would not have been possible without a fully integrated material management organization.

Results

At the completion of the five-year programme to achieve an integrated logistics strategy and management structure for Europe, the results were impressive. The results of the five-year materials management programme can be summarized as follows:

1 Customer service performance greatly improved; order fill rate which averaged 78 per cent in key markets in Europe in 1987 reached 98 per cent in 1993.
2 Logistics operations costs rose by less than inflation over the period and represented a smaller percentage of sales in all markets.
3 Despite an increase in SKUs of more than 50 per cent, an increased rate of new product launches and more sourcing of products from outside Europe, inventory levels had not risen.
4 Total materials management head-count was reduced in both warehouse operations and planning functions.

Source: Harland, David (1994) Achieving a Global Business: The Role of Logistics, *Logistics Focus*, 2, No. 7

Global logistics information systems

It will be apparent that to implement these ideas of flexible response through postponement and localization requires the

"Global visibility enables logistics management to better manage the flow of product"

ability to 'see' from one end of the pipeline to the other. Global visibility enables logistics management to better manage the flow of product and optimize production and transportation capacity whilst keeping inventory to a minimum.

Companies like Benetton are able to read demand on a daily basis from each of their worldwide markets and can plan production and delivery accordingly. They are aided in this by the advent of global logistics information capabilities provided by third party organizations like General Electric Information Services as well as in-house systems. Essentially, these systems enable sales to be monitored in real time, shipments to be tracked, purchase orders to be issued and production schedules to be monitored with the result that the 'pipeline' can be much better managed.

A significant benefit of achieving end-to-end pipeline visibility in a global context is the opportunities for improvement that become apparent once bottlenecks are highlighted and the inventory buffers – created as a result of lack of information – are revealed. For example, Toys 'R' Us, the US-based toy retailer, manages its product flow, from off-shore suppliers (mainly Far Eastern) into its world-wide retail outlets, literally from door-to-door. A third party global logistics service provider, APC, not only manages the transportation but through its tracking and tracing system is able to keep Toys 'R' Us informed of the precise location of every container and its contents. Information from the moment the product leaves the Asian factories is fed to the toy company so that two weeks before the cargo arrives, they can inform the retail stores of what is coming, potential delays and missing product, enabling stores to better manage their inventories and to re-order as necessary. Inventory savings are estimated to be in millions of dollars as a result.

Chapter checklist Serving the global customer: key issues

- The growth of the global corporation
  - Offshore sourcing and/or manufacturing
  - The rise of the global customer and the global brand
  - Rationalization and focusing the manufacturing/supply base

- Developing a global logistics strategy
  - Should we manage centrally or locally?
  - The search for global synergy
  - The basic question: to standardize or customize?

- Meeting local needs whilst seeking global economies
  - The opportunities for localization through 'postponement'
  - Where should inventory be carried?
  - Where should the forecast be made?

CHAPTER 7

Managing marketing logistics

Most managers work in organizations that are hierarchical, vertical and functional in their focus. The organization chart for the typical company resembles a pyramid and provides a clear view of where everyone fits in relation to each other and will also normally reflect reporting relationships. In essence, this conventional organization structure is little changed since the armies of the Roman Empire developed the precursor of today's organization.

Whilst there can be no doubt that this organizational model has served us well in the past, there are now serious questions about its appropriateness for the changed conditions that confront us today. Of the many changes that have taken place in the marketing environment, perhaps the biggest is the focus upon 'speed'. Because of shortening product life-cycles, time to market becomes ever more critical. Similarly the dramatic growth of JIT practices in manufacturing means that those companies wishing to supply into that environment have to develop systems capable of responding rapidly and flexibly to customers' delivery requirements. Indeed the same is true in almost every market today as organizations seek to reduce their inventories and hence a critical requirement of a supplier is that they are capable of rapid response.

The challenge to every business is to become a *responsive organization* in every sense of the word. The organization must respond to changes in the market with products and services which provide innovative solutions to customers' problems; it must respond to volatile demand and it must be able to provide high levels of flexibility in delivery.

What will be the distinguishing characteristics of the responsive organization? One thing is certain: it will not resemble today's functionally focused business. There will be many differences but the major transformations will probably be:

- from functions to processes
- from profit to performance
- from products to customers
- from vertical to virtual

Let us consider each of these in turn.

1 From functions to processes

Conventionally, organizations have been 'vertical' in their design. In other words, businesses have organized around functions such as production, marketing, sales and distribution. Each function has had clearly identified tasks and within these functional 'silos' or 'stovepipes' (as they have been called), there is a recognized hierarchy up which employees might hope to progress.

"Conventionally, organizations have been 'vertical' in their design"

The problem with this approach is that it is inwardly focused and concentrates primarily upon the use of resources rather than upon the creation of outputs. The outputs of any business can only be measured in terms of customer satisfaction achieved at a profit. Paradoxically, these outputs can only be achieved by coordination and cooperation *horizontally* across the organization. These horizontal linkages mirror the materials and information flows that link the customer with the business and its suppliers. They are in fact the *core processes* of the business. In the horizontal organization the emphasis is upon the management of processes.

"Processes are the fundamental tasks that have to be achieved in order to create and deliver customer value"

Processes are the fundamental tasks that have to be achieved in order to create and deliver customer value. In any business there are a number of core processes that should be managed on a cross-functional basis. Examples of core processes would include:

- brand development (including new product development)
- consumer development (primarily focused on building end-user loyalty)
- customer management (creating relationships with intermediaries)
- supplier development (strengthening up-stream relationships)
- supply chain management (including the order fulfilment process)

The transformation from a functional to a horizontal organization has major implications for the management structure of the business generally and for marketing management in particular.

In effect, in the horizontal organization marketing is no longer a series of activities performed within a marketing department. Indeed in many companies that have made the transition from vertical to horizontal organizations, the 'marketing department' has disappeared.

However, this is not to assume that marketing is dead; indeed the reverse is the case – the need for market driven businesses is as strong now as it ever was. Rather what we are seeing is the transformation of marketing from a narrow set of functional skills based upon a conventional '4 Ps' marketing mix, to a broader business orientation where the delivery of superior customer value becomes the key objective. However, this being said, it must be recognized that there are still important functional skills that marketing must continue to develop, for example, research to provide in-depth market understanding and knowledge of consumers' buying patterns, motivations and so forth.

Strategic marketing planning also takes on a different form in the horizontal organization. Essentially the task of marketing planning in this new organizational model is to translate strategic goals into *process* plans. For example, Guinness, a major brewing company, established the strategic goal of 'a perfect pint in every pub'. The marketing planning task in that company now becomes one of translating that goal into specific programmes for each process. So, for instance, what does 'a perfect pint in every pub' imply for the brand development process, the customer management process and so on? Because each process in this company is now managed by a cross-functional process team, a wider, more integrated perspective is brought to bear upon the issue.

"the task of marketing planning in this new organizational model is to translate strategic goals into process plans"

Guinness – in pursuit of the perfect pint

Guinness Plc is one of world's leading drinks companies, manufacturing and marketing a portfolio of best-selling spirits, together with a range of premium beers and lagers. Guinness Original stout, brewed by the company since the end of the eighteenth century, continues to be the brewing division's core brand

Guinness's products are distributed to every corner of the globe, but the UK continues to be the brewing division's single most important market. Beer consumption in the UK has been declining for many years, falling fastest in the traditional licensed trade sector (pubs and clubs). Unlike other UK breweries, Guinness owns none of the licensed premises through which its products are sold, and consequently it has no guaranteed outlets for its beers. Instead, it has successfully relied on consumer demand to persuade customers and competitors to stock its products. Guinness stout held its ground well within this declining market, but in the early 1990s competition stiffened with the launch of a number of rival stouts, and the rising popularity of imported bottled beers.

Across the industry, the fall in licensed sales has been partially off-set by growth in the take-home trade, but this brings little comfort to the brewers. Margins in the take-home trade are significantly lower than in the licensed trade sector, and the brewers are wary of falling hostage to the powerful retail chains.

The looming prospect of increased dependency on the take-home trade, intensified competition, and the growing complexity of Guinness's product portfolio, meant that costs had to be lowered and marketing effectiveness had to be improved to meet the rigours of the changing environment. The brewer was forced to re-examine the way it managed and organized its marketing activities within the organization as a whole. 'Project Condor', a programme to improve the market-place focus of Guinness Brewing, was the result.

Launched in 1994, Project Condor aimed to engineer a shift away from Guinness's traditional functional focus towards a process orientation, reducing the number of 'functional fingers in the pie' – each building cost and delay into the operation. Improving quality and speed were therefore seen as integral objectives, so was a substantial reduction in the number of staff in the brewing, marketing and administrative functions.

Marketing at Guinness Brewing had hitherto been organized on a product management basis, with separate sales and marketing functions. Under Project Condor the old marketing and sales organizations were slimmed down and restructured around two new 'demand companies' – Guinness Brewing GB 'On Trade' and 'Off Trade' – plus a 'consumer marketing' group. The two 'demand companies' took over responsibility for sales and marketing management within their respective sectors, and for their customers' and their sectors' profitability. The new consumer marketing group handled brand management and had wider corporate profitability responsibilities. Inevitably some overlapping and competing interests remained, but the reorganization facilitated further efforts to improve performance on three strategic dimensions. The first is product leadership. Guinness believed that the future of its business was heavily dependent on product excellence, given that it owned none of its retail outlets. Second was customer intimacy, through greater concentration on the specific needs of distinct customer groups. Third was operational excellence, which would become even more critical with growing dependency on the low-return take-home business.

Operation Condor put other infrastructural changes in place within the business. Not least the move from standard to activity based costing (ABC). Though hampered by the slow and expensive task of an IT upgrade and the initial reluctance of the accounts department, the adoption of ABC quickly proved its worth. Investment decisions had always been made around the core brand, but it was anticipated that the peripheral brands could become more important if competition in the black beer sector continued to increase. Standard costing methods indicated that new brands were very profitable, but Guinness quickly discovered that previously hidden costs surfaced with the application of ABC. Under the new system the set-up costs of a new brand were factored into the equation, so were the costs incurred through increased complexity. Suddenly the core brand, Draught Guinness, appeared to be relatively more profitable than anyone had realized.

Draught Guinness had a loyal following among older drinkers, and a five-year advertising campaign starring Rutger Hauer as the 'Man with the Guinness' had successfully positioned it as a quirky premium brand in the minds of younger drinkers. But the 'pure genius' of the advertising could not alone turn curious or occasional drinkers into loyal customers. The product itself had to meet the consumer's expectations if they were going to try it for a second time, and hopefully acquire a taste for the thick dark beer. Worryingly though, it seemed that all too often the customer was presented with a less than perfect pint.

Guinness had just completed a £50 million brewery upgrade, and a quality audit established that the draught beer left the brewery in prime condition. Things were going awry somewhere downstream, but no-one knew exactly where. Remedying the problem fell beyond the remit of any single department at Guinness, so a cross-functional team was assembled to work on a solution. The rest of the product delivery process – from brewery to consumer – was studied, mapped and measured. The problems, it transpired, developed once the beer arrived at the licensed premises. Licensees did not always observe the brewer's recommendations for storage and presentation, and whilst both were beyond the direct control of Guinness, they were essential to the delivered quality of the product.

A plan was drawn up, outlining a programme which they believed, when implemented, would consistently deliver 'the perfect pint'. Consideration was given to resourcing, training, communications, with key performance indicators identified and internal service levels agreements arranged at each step in the supply chain. The programme's progress was measured weekly, and its results communicated within Guinness's brewing division. Although Guinness had not purposefully developed cross-functional team working in the past, the foundations for such an approach had been laid two years earlier with 'Breakthrough'. Breakthrough was an internal marketing and communication programme which at the time aimed to align all employees behind the company's strategic objectives. The programme had a lasting effect, and the internal communications team established as part of the Breakthrough initiative became an important link in the perfect pint project.

To deliver the perfect pint, draught Guinness should be stored and served at a temperature of between 5–8°C, served in a straight 'Guinness' glass, and topped with a tight creamy head 10–15mm deep. To achieve the desired result, the pint had to be dispensed in a two parts, allowing most of the beer to settle for a minute before topping up the glass. Old established users' pubs already used the two-part pour, but other establishments needed a little more help. First the actual pouring process was made easier by the development and installation of special founts, at a total cost of £70,000. A technical field team was created and despatched, once the devices were installed, to train the licensees. After training the licensees received perfect pint training certificates together with a range of two-part pour promotional material. These included instruction cards detailing the two-part pour technique, and exchange cards which – after a number of recorded purchases – could be redeemed by the consumer in exchange for Guinness merchandise (T-shirts, lapel pins, etc.). A television advertising campaign was commissioned to support the initiative, a version of which was also released on the Internet and quickly became a cult screen save.

Guinness Original stout went on to achieve its highest ever share of the total draught beer market. The process management approach used to deliver the perfect pint was so successful that Guinness Brewing has used cross-functional teams to identify and streamline other key business processes including order handling (order to cash), new product and packaging development, and category management.

Source: Presentation by Julian Spooner, Marketing Director, Guinness Brewing GB, Cranfield School of Management, January 1996

Some might argue that this underpinning, integrative process of strategic marketing planning might better be termed strategic business planning. This is really only semantic and in reality it does not matter what we call this critical process, only that we manage it and recognize its central importance.

"processes are in effect 'capabilities' and it is through capabilities that the organization competes"

The justification for this radically different view of the business is that these processes are in effect 'capabilities' and it is through capabilities that the organization competes. In other words the effectiveness of the new product development process, the order fulfilment process and so on determines the extent to which the business will succeed in the market place. Hence the need to manage capabilities and not just functions.

It was earlier suggested that the competitiveness of an organization is increasingly based upon its capabilities and competencies and that the way it manages the under-pinning 'core-processes' is critical. A process in an organizational context may be defined as:

Any activity or group of activities that takes an input, adds value to it, and provides an output to an internal or external customer.

The characteristics of business processes include:

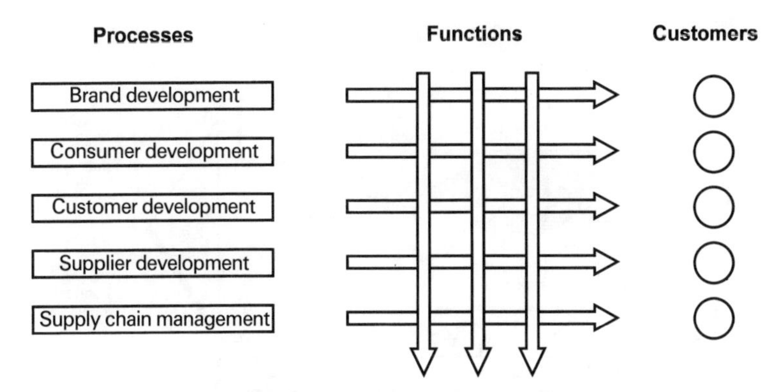

Figure 7.1 Managing cross-functional processes to create customer value

- They have customers for whom they create value.
- They typically cross functional boundaries.
- They draw upon functional resources.
- They are team-based.
- They have strategic goals.

The challenge to the organization is to break down the vertical, functional barriers to integration and instead to become a horizontal, market-facing business. The driving force for this change is the realization that it is processes that create customer value, not functions.

Managing the processes that deliver customer value is the key to market-place success. The shift from functional management to process management is summarized in Figure 7.1.

"Managing the processes that deliver customer value is the key to market-place success"

In the process-oriented organization, cross-functional teams are charged with achieving business goals defined in terms of customer value and customer profitability. This represents a radical shift from the traditional organization that focused around functional management and where the means of satisfying customer requirements was via a series of 'hand-offs' from one function to another.

Under this revised organizational model the role of functional management is now quite different. Essentially it is to create 'pools of resource' or 'centres of excellence' from which process teams will draw their members. Unipart, a UK-based company in the automotive industry has gone so far as to re-name its traditional functions as 'schools', the idea being that they should become centres of functional excellence, the major purpose of which is to provide training and development for process team members.

Managing cross-functional processes is becoming a critical source of competitive advantage

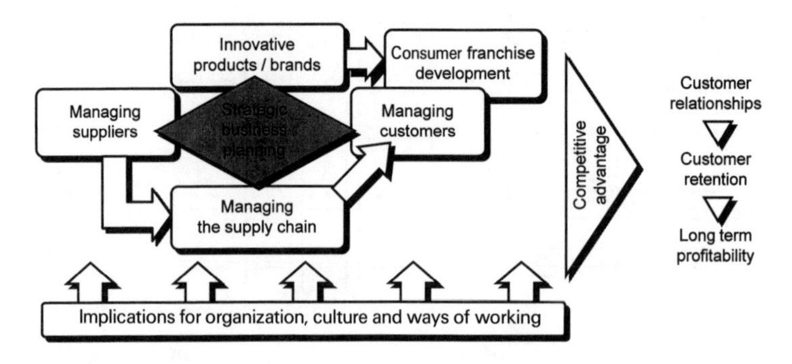

Supply chain processes aligned with customers' and suppliers' processes

Figure 7.2 Superior business processes

One of the most significant advantages of process teams is that they are customer facing and that, as a result, they tend to focus on ways in which opportunities can be created for further value enhancement. In particular by focusing upon 'customer satisfaction' in its broadest sense there is the inevitable recognition that marketing and logistics are irrevocably inter-twinned. Figure 7.2 suggests a revised organizational model that focuses upon the processes that directly or indirectly deliver customer satisfaction.

Businesses that wish to become market-facing must by definition shift their orientation from the vertical to the horizontal. By this is meant that they must find ways of managing across functions and coordinating all of the previously separate activities from procurement through to distribution. Since customer satisfaction at a profit is the over-riding aim of any commercial organization, management of the 'customer satisfaction process' should be the priority.

To manage this radically different type of business will need a new set of skills and managerial capabilities. Interestingly, the emerging profession of logistics management is providing a key source of people capable of working in a cross-functional environment. By its very nature, logistics is an integrative, coordinating activity, and the managers who work in it tend to be well versed in the art of managing across functions. Logistics managers understand customer service, they understand the trade-off opportunities in distribution, they understand requirements planning and the need for procurement to be linked to the factory and beyond that to the warehouse. These same managers are accustomed to working in teams, they have facilitation and communication skills. In addition they understand the opportunities that information technology can provide as the driving force for breaking down the functional barriers.

All this is not to suggest that the transition to the horizontal organization will be straightforward. Layers of existing management may no longer be necessary, territories will be broken up, evaluating and rewarding individual performance will not be as straightforward in the new team-based business and nothing will remain the same for long in an organization that seeks to respond to a changing environment.

2 From profit to performance

Whilst there can be no arguing that long-term, sustained profit has to be the goal of any commercial organization, there is a growing realization that if profit is the *end*, then we should spend more time examining the *means* whereby it is achieved. So many management boards begin their weekly meetings with a review of the financial position. In other words, before anything else gets discussed, revenues will be examined and costs detailed at some length. Ratios, capacity utilization, production efficiencies – these are the currency by which the business is measured and hence controlled.

There is a saying that 'what gets measured, gets managed', implying that it is through the choice of performance measurement that behaviour is determined. Thus, in a business where employees are required to 'clock' in and out of work each day, punctuality may be improved but their willingness to work more than the agreed hours may be reduced. Hence the importance of understanding what the critical performance criteria are and thus what we should be measuring.

The underlying logic of this viewpoint is that performance drives profitability – if we get the right performance then profit will follow.

"performance drives profitability"

Many of these new performance indicators will be non-financial. That is, they will focus management's attention upon such things as customer satisfaction, flexibility and employee commitment. The management meetings of the near future may begin their agenda not with the financial review – that will come later – but with a review of such non-financial performance indicators as:

Customer satisfaction:

- Customer retention
- Brand preference
- Dealer satisfaction
- Service performance

Flexibility:

- Set-up times
- Commonality of components and materials
- Throughput times
- Percentage value-added time

People commitment:

- Employee turnover
- Suggestions submitted and implemented
- Internal service climate and culture
- Training and development index

Within each individual organization the key performance indicators will necessarily be different but the principle of focusing upon the drivers of profitability is paramount.

One performance measure that has attracted a lot of interest recently is the concept of 'economic value added' (EVA). EVA is simply the difference between the company's net operating profit after taxes and the cost of capital. If the difference is positive, the company is creating wealth for its shareholders, if negative it is destroying wealth! Whilst it is a simple concept, it is not always fully understood. Sometimes the true cost of capital is under-estimated. Properly speaking, the cost of capital to an organization is the weighted average cost of its debt and its equity. The cost of its debt is easy to identify, but the cost of equity is more debatable. The appropriate cost concept to use here is 'opportunity cost' – what return could the shareholder get elsewhere – with some adjustment for the 'riskiness' of the business.

Also, too, the definition of capital employed should be broadened to include R&D, intellectual capital and brand building activity.

Once the concept of EVA is accepted and understood within the organization it can then be applied to the various activities of the business, for example, serving different markets or distribution channels. It is particularly helpful in measuring logistics performance. Shortening end-to-end pipeline time for instance can significantly improve EVA by reducing the inventory in the pipeline whilst simultaneously reducing costs. Similarly programmes which focus on improving 'perfect order' achievement build EVA by minimizing invoice queries and adjustments hence reducing accounts receivable.

Using 'activity based costing' (ABC) to understand the true costs of processes can provide a further basis for establishing performance indicators in logistics. In particular, ABC can help identify the real costs of serving different customers and as a result focus attention upon ways in which the order fulfilment process can be amended to improve EVA.

A vital element in process improvement is *benchmarking*. By examining in detail how other organizations create value for their customers and how they manage the value-creation processes, we can learn a great deal about our own processes. Benchmarking, properly performed, reveals inefficiencies in well-established processes. As a result of a successful benchmarking programme many questions will be raised about how our current processes are structured and managed.

"Benchmarking, properly performed, reveals inefficiencies in well-established processes"

Whatever tools and techniques may be used, the fundamental question is: are we measuring the right things and using the appropriate metrics? Conventional measures have tended to measure functional performance and to be focused upon efficiency, e.g. capacity utilization, cost per case and so on. Process-oriented measures, on the other hand, emphasize such things as customer satisfaction, throughput times, cost-to-serve and other similar measures.

3 From products to customers

Even though the marketing concept has gained widespread acceptance across industry there is still an underlying tendency to manage products rather than customers. This emphasis is reflected in job titles such as 'brand manager', 'product group manager' and in accounting systems that can provide precise information on product profitability but that are incapable of measuring the profitability of customers.

Because customer satisfaction has to be the ultimate objective of any commercial organization it is imperative that the management structures and the measurement systems also mirror this. In organizational terms the requirement is to create a means whereby markets, channels and customers can be managed and appropriate accounting and control procedures can be implemented. 'Demand management' is emerging now in some leading edge companies as an integrating, cross-functional approach to servicing customers.

Such approaches need to be supported by accounting systems that can better identify the costs of servicing customers and hence their profitability. In the same way that 20 per cent of a company's products will generate 80 per cent of its profits, so too do 20 per cent of its customers generate 80 per cent of the profit. The problem in the past has been that traditional accounting systems have not been able to provide accurate measures of the 'costs-to-serve'. Now, using activity based costing and throughput costing, it is possible to identify the aspects of service that create cost and hence, where necessary, to modify the service package customer by customer.

As was suggested in Chapter 3, this transformation will also need a greater emphasis on 'customer value' and not just 'brand value'. Essentially this means that the supplying organization must focus its efforts upon developing an 'offer' or 'package' that will positively impact customers' perceptions of the value that they derive through ownership of that offer. The argument that is increasingly being voiced is that a critical component of such customer value is service. In a sense we are approaching the time when logistics and marketing need to be managed conjointly.

"we are approaching the time when logistics and marketing need to be managed conjointly"

Traditionally, the major focus of marketing – at least in consumer markets – has been upon the end user and upon the development of brand loyalty. However, of late there has been a growing recognition of the importance of building relationships with marketing and distribution intermediaries who may often control the access to the end user or consumer. These intermediaries could be retailers, distributors, stockists or wholesalers or indeed original equipment manufacturers (OEMs). Without their support and cooperation it is becoming increasingly difficult to achieve success in the final market place. As a result, many companies are now re-focusing their marketing strategies to place a greater emphasis upon the development and management of customer relationships.

To a certain extent the shift in the balance of power away from the supplier to the customer is forcing a re-appraisal of traditional trading arrangements. Even allowing for this however, there are strong arguments from the standpoint of competitive advantage for seeking closer relationships with customers. One of the key reasons for wishing to achieve 'preferred supplier' status is the obvious one that it provides a strong barrier to entry to potential competitors. For instance, in the first year that Procter & Gamble forged a supply chain relationship with Wal-Mart in the USA they increased their sales through that outlet by 40 per cent. Much of the additional shelf space they gained came from competitive brands.

Outside of the retail environment, similar opportunities exist for enhancing customer value. 'Key account management' is increasingly replacing classic sales management as customers grow in size and hence in purchasing power. Now the issue is to find ways in which the supplying company can enhance the profitability of the customer's business. In other words, rather than focus on selling products to customers, focus instead on creating value for customers. For example, in the offshore oil exploration and production business it is now not unusual to find suppliers to the exploration and production companies providing a range of value-adding services on a 'one-stop' shopping basis. So, for instance, a large integrated supplier such as Brown and Root or Foster Wheeler will manage the inventories of spares and consumables for customers such as Conoco or Chevron on the basis of shared information on usage.

Key account management is also increasingly team-based and cross-functional to facilitate the search for opportunities to create customer value. Some companies such as Kraft and Procter & Gamble have replaced product-based divisional sales forces with cross-functional teams to relate to major accounts.

Figure 7.3 shows how at Kraft customer teams are supported by category teams and process teams so that an integrated business-wide approach may be adopted for all major accounts.

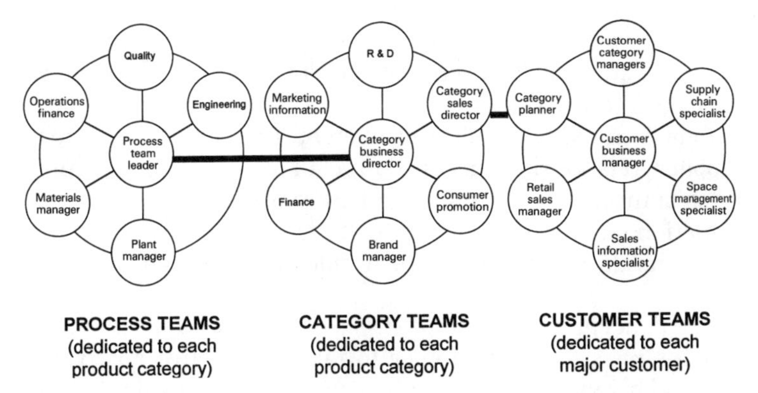

Figure 7.3 Managing through teams at Kraft. *Source*: George, M., Freeling, A. and Court, D. (1994) Reinventing the Marketing Organization, *McKinsey Quarterly*, No. 4. © 1994 McKinsey & Company. All rights reserved

4 From vertical to virtual

In previous years a favoured organization model was that of 'vertical' integration whereby the company would seek to control through ownership its upstream suppliers and/or its downstream customers. Companies like Courtaulds in textiles or General Motors in automobiles typified this approach.

Whilst some companies have undoubtedly benefited from the access to low-cost materials or guaranteed markets, the generally held view today is that organizations may do better to focus just on their 'core business' or 'core competencies' and to outsource everything else. This latter model requires a different sort of integration with suppliers of these outsourced activities. It is an integration that is likely to be based upon the sharing of information and the creation of common strategic goals. This is the concept of 'virtual' integration or, as some have called it, the 'virtual corporation'.

"organizations may do better to focus just on their 'core business' or 'core competencies'"

If this trend towards outsourcing continues, then a critical competitive differentiator will be the skill with which the network is managed and coordinated. Network competition requires a different approach to managing supply chain relationships.

The traditional supplier/buyer relationship has often been described as 'adversarial'. The position adopted in the past was that the aim of purchasing management is to seek to minimize the costs of supply whilst ensuring requisite quality. In the conventional model this is achieved by seeking to encourage competition amongst suppliers – particularly on price. Indeed, it has often been a case of 'playing one off against the other'. Again, it was always thought to be good policy to have more than one supplier for each item purchased to avoid 'placing all the eggs in one basket'.

Today's thinking is radically different. The aim is to seek to use supplier relationships as a source of competitive advantage. Since competitive advantage derives to a large extent from cost reduction and/or differentiation, it is only logical that these goals should be the driver for a different approach to supplier relations.

The concept of *supplier development* proposes that it is in the best interests of the customer to take a proactive approach to the establishment of a mutually beneficial relationship with suppliers. In other words, customers should actively seek to find ways in which they can work together with suppliers to both reduce the total costs of ownership whilst constantly seeking to enhance further their own differentiation through such means as improved quality, innovative design, unique technologies – all of which will be strongly influenced by supplier involvement.

In the automobile industry this approach has found many advocates and there has been a marked swing away from the 'adversarial' model to the 'partnership' model. A company like Rover, now part of BMW, has adopted this concept and now talks in terms of the 'extended enterprise'. The implication is that the suppliers' processes should be integrated as closely as possible with Rover's. In this way a 'seamless' pipeline can be created which not only makes for greater efficiency through reduced paperwork, lower inventory and faster response, but also creates an environment in which the search for continual cost reduction and value enhancement becomes a priority.

Managing supplier relationships not only entails a fundamental shift in attitudes on both sides, but also a recognition that partnership does not imply a weakening in the desire to improve performance. Indeed, successful partnerships in the supply chain tend to be based very much on hard commercial realities. A good example is provided by Marks & Spencer (M&S), the United Kingdom's most profitable retailer, and their major clothing supplier, Coats Viyella. To quote Coats Viyella's chief executive, Neville Bain:

> *being a supplier of M&S is a true partnership. Meeting the rigorous standards M&S demand isn't easy because it covers every dimension of the business. However, the shared commitment, and shared financial gains have enabled Coats to invest heavily in information technology, particularly Computer Aided Design, to link customer and supplier.*

Source: Susan Gilchrist, 'Stores aim to reclaim buried pots of gold' *The Times*, London, 6 September 1994.
© Times Newspapers Ltd 1994

Coats Viyella has direct electronic links between its design studio and M&S so that designs can be viewed, and, if necessary changed by both parties on screen. The same source quoted the joint managing director of M&S as saying:

> *We will be building on our supplier partnerships with links that enable operational data to be shared across the supply chain. The network will enable us to bring new merchandise to market more quickly. More than ever before, what we sell today will influence what we deliver tomorrow and what we produce next week.*

Similar examples of the contribution of supplier/buyer partnerships are increasingly encountered in a multitude of industries, suggesting that the age of network competition has begun.

We conclude this chapter with an example of a logistics alliance between Laura Ashley, the international retailer, and Federal Express. In 1990, Laura Ashley faced significant financial problems in large part due to its inability to manage its global supply chain. Federal Express was able to provide Laura Ashley with a logistics capability which they would have had great difficulty creating on their own. The Laura Ashley/Fedex alliance provides an example of how logistics partnerships have the potential to become a powerful source of competitive advantage in this new world of network competition.

Laura Ashley: improving capabilities through strategic alliances

In February 1990, international fashion and furnishings group Laura Ashley announced year-end losses of £4.7m on a turnover of £296m, with debts of £89m. Difficult trading conditions across several key markets, crippling interest payments and order processing problems were cited in the 1990 annual report as the cause of the company's difficulties. Days later, the banks were called in, following the breach of a loan covenant. Refinancing was agreed, but the banks demanded improvements in operations. In particular something had to be done about the company's appalling logistics performance. At year end Laura Ashley had £105m tied up in stock, yet it could not deliver to its shops on time. The problems were particularly acute in North America, where that year's autumn/winter clothes collection had arrived approximately three months late, resulting in immediate mark-downs.

When new CEO Jim Maxmin moved into post in September 1991, logistics concerns were top of the agenda. Laura Ashley had a sizeable in-house distribution department operating five major warehouses around the globe, using a total of ten largely unconnected management information systems. There were no less than eight principal linehaul carriers, and a multitude of other transport suppliers, to serve 555 stores in 28 countries.

The warehouses were holding over 55,000 lines of inventory (though only around 15,000 were current stock), ranging from

35 metre rolls of fabric, through to wedding gowns, wooden furniture, and tins of paint. Only 5 per cent of lines were common to all stores. Delivery systems were hopelessly clogged, with overall stock availability at around 80 per cent.

There were problems with the order processing systems too. A sale recorded by the EPOS system would automatically trigger a replenishment order. The system was programmed to give priority to the larger stores, but made no allowances for the speed at which goods sold, or the urgency of the order. Large London shops would be replenished on a daily basis, whether the stock was selling quickly or not, but a small regional store which sold its entire allocation of an item within a day, might be left for weeks with a total stockout. Another flaw in the system was that it did not distinguish between real sales and goods redirected to other stores.

In the UK, the company resorted to handing out £25 vouchers to placate frustrated customers whose orders stubbornly refused to arrive. Laura Ashley's logistics and management information systems were clearly in need of urgent attention, but the company had neither the time or expertise to develop them in-house, so Maxmin turned to cooperative suppliers for help.

In March 1992, Laura Ashley and Federal Express Business Logistics jointly announced that they had formed a 'global alliance'. Together they would restructure and manage the flow of goods and information within the Laura Ashley supply chain. The alliance, agreed in principle during a telephone call from Maxmin to a long-standing business contact at Federal Express, took five months to finalize. Under the terms of the agreement, Laura Ashley turned over its entire logistics operation to its new partner. This was an open-book agreement, with both parties sharing financial and strategic planning information. It would run for an indefinite period (minimum of 10 years), and would be worth an estimated £150m to Federal Express. In return they would supply the logistics and stock management systems that Laura Ashley so desperately needed, upgrading its capabilities almost immediately, and reducing its operating costs in the longer term. Products could be delivered quickly and efficiently via Federal Express's own global air network, thus enabling Laura Ashley to reduce its cripplingly high stock levels, while significantly improving the quality of its customer service.

The same spirit of partnership and long-term cooperation was evident when Laura Ashley signed a multi-million pound deal with ICL. The Anglo-Japanese computer company would progressively upgrade Laura Ashley's management information systems. In addition it assigned 10 members of staff to coordinate the project from Laura Ashley's offices in Maidenhead.

Maxmin was aware that questions hung over the wisdom and cost effectiveness of these type of arrangements, and that alliances themselves are rarely established without significant teething troubles. Nevertheless he was convinced that the long-term benefits – for all parties – outweighed the short-term financial gains of dealing with suppliers of essential services on a transactional basis.

Chapter checklist Managing marketing logistics: key issues

- The need for organizational change
  - From functions to processes
  - From profit to performance
  - From products to customers
  - From vertical to virtual

- Manage processes, not just functions
  - Processes are competitive capabilities
  - Processes require functional excellence to support them
  - Processes create customer value

- What gets measured gets managed
  - The importance of performance measurement
  - Use non-financial performance indicators
  - Focus on internal and external customer satisfaction

Index